# MAKE TROUBLE

## Standing Up, Speaking Out, and Finding the Courage to Lead

### CECILE RICHARDS
#### WITH LAUREN PETERSON

YOUNG READERS EDITION
adapted by Ruby Shamir

Margaret K. McElderry Books
New York  London  Toronto  Sydney  New Delhi

MARGARET K. McELDERRY BOOKS

An imprint of Simon & Schuster Children's Publishing Division

1230 Avenue of the Americas, New York, New York 10020

This work is a memoir. It reflects the author's present recollections of her experiences over a period of years.

Text copyright © 2018, 2019 by Cecile Richards

This young readers edition is adapted from *Make Trouble* by Cecile Richards, published by Touchstone in 2018.

Cover illustrations copyright © 2019 by Eugenia Mello

Cover lettering copyright © 2019 by Yani&Guille

All rights reserved, including the right of reproduction in whole or in part in any form.

MARGARET K. McELDERRY BOOKS is a trademark of Simon & Schuster, Inc.

For information about special discounts for bulk purchases, please contact Simon & Schuster Special Sales at 1-866-506-1949 or business@simonandschuster.com.

The Simon & Schuster Speakers Bureau can bring authors to your live event. For more information or to book an event, contact the Simon & Schuster Speakers Bureau at 1-866-248-3049 or visit our website at www.simonspeakers.com.

Also available in a Margaret K. McElderry Books hardcover edition

Interior design by Vikki Sheatsley

Cover design by Lauren Rille

The text for this book was set in Simoncini Garamond.

Manufactured in the United States of America

1121 MTN

First Margaret K. McElderry Books paperback edition October 2020

10 9 8 7 6 5 4 3 2

The Library of Congress has cataloged the hardcover edition as follows:

Names: Richards, Cecile, author. | Peterson, Lauren (Lauren Collins), author. | Shamir, Ruby, author.

Title: Make trouble : standing up, speaking out, and finding the courage to lead / Cecile Richards with Lauren Peterson.

Description: Young readers edition / adapted by Ruby Shamir. | New York : Margaret K. McElderry Books, [2019] | Includes index. | Audience: Ages 10 up. | Audience: Grades 7-9. | Summary: "To make change, you have to make trouble. Cecile Richards has been fighting for what she believes in ever since she was taken to the principal's office in seventh grade for wearing an armband in protest of the Vietnam War. She had an extraordinary childhood in ultra-conservative Texas, where her father, a civil rights attorney, and her mother, an avid activist and the first female governor of Texas, taught their kids to be troublemakers. From the time Richards was a girl, she had a front row seat to observe the rise of women in American politics. And by sharing her story with young readers, she shines a light on the people and lessons that have gotten her though good times and bad, and encourages her audience to take risks, make mistakes, and make trouble along the way."—Provided by publisher.

Identifiers: LCCN 2019023588 (print) | ISBN 9781534451957 (hardcover) | ISBN 9781534451964 (paperback) | ISBN 9781534451971 (eBook)

Subjects: LCSH: Richards, Cecile—Juvenile literature. | Women political activists—United States— Biography—Juvenile literature. | Leadership in women—United States—History—Juvenile literature. | Women's rights—United States—History—Juvenile literature. | Social justice—United States— History—Juvenile literature.

Classification: LCC HQ1236.5.U6 R53 2019 (print) | DDC 320.082/0973—dc23

LC record available at https://lccn.loc.gov/2019023588

LC eBook record available at https://lccn.loc.gov/201902358

*To Kirk, Hannah, Daniel, and Lily.*
*And to Mom and Dad*
*for getting this whole party started.*

# Contents

---

# INTRODUCTION

ittle lady, you are just trying to make trouble."

That was my sixth-grade teacher, Mrs. Powers, at University Park Elementary School in Dallas, Texas. She had spent the past fifteen minutes conducting an interrogation: Why was I refusing to recite the Lord's Prayer with the rest of the class?

I'm not even sure I knew that it was unconstitutional to have us start each day with the Lord's Prayer. Thanks to the First Amendment to the US Constitution, we don't practice religion in public school. But by God, my class did, right after the Pledge of Allegiance. That morning, though, I didn't want to. When Mrs. Powers asked me why I wasn't participating, I said calmly, "We don't read the Bible in my house." Mrs. Powers's eyes flew open. I could see from her stricken look that she had taken my honesty for rudeness. I suppose in a way it was.

My family wasn't religious, not in a traditional sense,

but we did go to the Unitarian church, which was a home away from home for families like ours in Dallas—our own little bunker in the middle of the crazy culture war of the 1960s, and the heart of the local anti–Vietnam War movement. Folks in our congregation were involved in everything from organizing workers to form unions, to the local radical newspaper, which my dad happened to be defending in court. Religion was cool with me; it just didn't include the Lord's Prayer. It was pretty obvious from Mrs. Powers's reaction what she thought about that. There was no hope for me; clearly I was headed for a life of crime.

Up until then I was the classic all-A's first child. I lived to make my parents proud of me, which meant sticking to certain rules. I was the kid who never got in trouble—a trait that annoyed my younger brother Dan to no end. But the shame and humiliation of being called out in front of my class by Mrs. Powers was an eye-opener. In that moment I realized something: my parents weren't the only ones who didn't fit into the buttoned-up, conservative Dallas culture. I didn't fit in either.

It was the first time I remember having to decide: Do I accept things the way they are, or do I question authority? I chose the latter, and from that point forward I was branded a troublemaker. I wore the designation like a badge of honor. I've been making trouble ever since—which, to me, means taking on the powers that be, being a thorn in someone's side, standing up to injustice, or just plain raising hell, with a very clear set of values as my guide.

Sometimes being a troublemaker can be pretty awesome.

After all, it was one of the great troublemakers of all time, Emma Goldman, who said, "If I can't dance, I don't want to be part of your revolution." Other times it's scary and carries big risks—the risk of losing your friends, your reputation, your job, or all of the above.

Over the years I've had the good fortune to meet trouble-makers from all walks of life: nursing-home workers in East Texas, janitors in Los Angeles, members of Congress, organizers and activists of every age on the front lines of the struggle for justice. I watched in awe as my mother, Ann Richards, went from frustrated housewife to governor of Texas, against all odds. That was one of the things that drew me to Planned Parenthood, the provider of women's health care I ran for twelve years: its history is the history of brave, troublemaking women (and a few good men) who risked their reputations and even their lives to change things. We fellow travelers have a way of finding each other, whether we set out to or not.

This book is the story of the people who have taught me about mustering the courage and defiance to fight injustice, because it can be really hard to do when people in the world like Mrs. Powers make you feel small. The truth is, anything worth doing has its challenges. Hopefully, these stories will inspire you to think how you might bring about change in your neighborhood or even in the wider world. And, yes, fighting for what you believe in can be discouraging, defeating, and sometimes downright depressing. But it can also be powerful, inspiring, fun, and funny—and it can introduce you to people who will change your life. That's the message I want to spread far and wide. That's why I wrote this book.

I started my career organizing women who were working too hard for too little money to start a union so they could stand up to their powerful employers. In different jobs, I have figured out that there are countless ways to do what is right and help all people live a full and decent life.

Can you be an activist? Of course you can—whether it's the work you do for a living when you grow up or whether it ends up as more of an extracurricular activity on the side. But you don't have to wait that long—you can start right now. Maybe you care about families who live in poverty and are struggling to get by, or maybe you worry about making sure that none of your classmates ever go hungry. Maybe you're concerned about the endangered animals that are threatened by our rapidly warming planet, or maybe you want your school and neighborhood to be safe from gun violence. I hope this book will inspire you to get out there and do something about it, to resist policies that hurt our communities and fight for those that help. In my lifetime, these causes have been most often championed by the Democratic Party. They've been labeled progressive, liberal, left-wing, or even radical. But it's never seemed radical to me that everyone deserves an equal shot to thrive and a seat at the table. The Republican Party, especially the far right wing, has often opposed these causes. So we fight. Not using violence, but using our voices and our votes. Sometimes justice comes when we knock on doors, make phone calls, and persuade people to cast a ballot. Sometimes that's not enough. Just don't forget: to make a difference, you have to make a little trouble.

# Raised to Make Trouble

I've been training for the resistance my whole life. I was raised by troublemakers. Neither of my parents ever backed away from a righteous fight.

My father, David Richards, is a civil rights attorney whose career has been rabble-rousing. And Mom? When she was coming up in Waco, Texas, girls were expected to set their sights no further than the home—they should grow up to become good wives and mothers. Mom rebelled against those expectations and willed herself to become the first woman elected in her own right as governor of Texas. She believed she was put on this earth to make a difference.

My folks grew up in the hard-core Baptist environment of Waco, high school sweethearts from different sides of town. Mom's parents were country folk from humble beginnings who worked long and hard for everything they had. They were survivors of the Great Depression of the 1930s, when millions of Americans lost their jobs and their homes and went hungry. Her father—Cecil, for whom I'm named—traveled to small-town drugstores throughout central and western Texas selling medicines. Poppy, as I called him, was well over six feet tall, with a gentle way about him. He never graduated from high school, yet his street smarts and keen sense of people made him a natural salesman. He always had some hilarious way of stating the obvious. "That's no hill for a stepper" was a favorite. In other words, "You can overcome anything if you're determined."

Mom's mother also had little in the way of formal schooling. But she knew how to fend for herself and her family; she made my mother's clothes and grew and canned all her own vegetables—survival skills I'm so grateful she passed along to me. There was never a moment when the deep freezer in the garage didn't have enough food to survive a nuclear holocaust.

Nona was no-nonsense and did not suffer fools. The day my mother was born, going to the hospital was unthinkable; they didn't have the money, and giving birth at home was just the country way. When Nona went into labor, she called a neighbor woman to come over and cook for Cecil, as it was unimaginable that he would make his own dinner that night. The story goes that the neighbor was struggling to kill the chicken that was planned for his meal, so my grandmother hoisted herself up on one elbow, reached out her other hand, and wrung that chicken's neck right there from the birthing bed. Mom told that story every chance she got. "Mama is tough," she'd say with a mix of pride and awe. "She isn't scared of anything."

Mom and Dad, age sixteen, as Dad gets shipped off from Waco, Texas, to Andover.

Dad's parents were on the other end of the social spectrum from Mom's. They were Waco society and belonged to the Ridgewood Country Club. They traveled the globe when that was unheard-of in Texas, and it was my grandmother Eleanor who later introduced me to the world. Worried that their only son would fall in love at such a young age with a Waco girl, they shipped my father off to a prep school in Massachusetts, in hopes of breaking up the romance. It didn't work. My dad rebelled and soon was back at Waco High and back with my mom.

My parents married in 1953 after their junior year of college. After my dad graduated from law school, he took a job with a Dallas law firm known for representing labor unions, which support the rights of workers to band together for decent pay and working conditions and even to stop work, or strike, if they aren't treated fairly.

Dad also took up civil rights cases, to ensure that all people were equally protected under the law, no matter the color of their skin. There weren't a lot of lawyers doing this kind of work in Texas at the time.

Around then Mom realized she was pregnant with me. And after me came my brothers, Dan and Clark, and later my sister, Ellen. We spent our early years in Dallas, in a house on Lovers Lane. It was small and cramped for the six of us, but Mom spent long hours decorating to try to make it look like the Dallas homes she'd seen in magazine photos.

In those days, women in our neighborhood were expected to stay home, take care of the family, and help make their husbands successful. Mom pursued her role as a housewife with purpose. While Dad was working on "a big, important case," she baked our birthday cakes from scratch and tried every latest recipe. On Easter she'd have us dye dozens of eggs, wrap hundreds of jelly beans in plastic wrap, and throw the biggest Easter egg hunt around. At Christmas she put up the tallest, most elaborately decorated tree. As she once said, "If it was in a glossy magazine, I was doing it!"

People often say to me, "It must have been incredible to have Ann Richards as a mom!" And of course it was. But to paint the picture a bit more clearly, it was not as if this young mother, the only child of working-class parents, sprang fully formed as a sharp-witted, feminist icon. That happened over

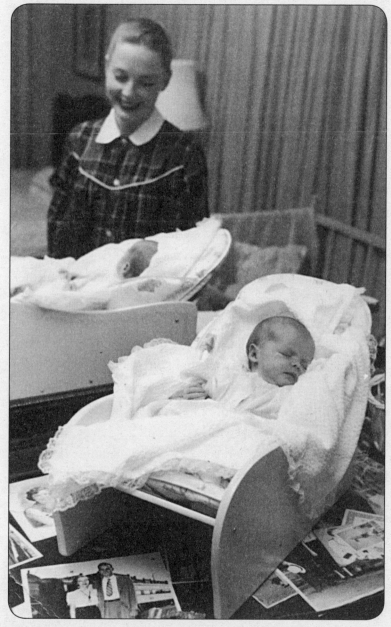

Mom and me in her childhood bedroom.

the course of many years. But even early on, I could see that
Mom was quietly beginning to revolt against the role she was
expected to play. I suspect it was those early days in Dallas,
being the perfect wife and mother, that set the stage for her
rebellion later on.

Life in Dallas back then is hard to imagine unless you
experienced it. The city was segregated, drawing a deep and
unjust divide between African Americans and whites. Racism was rampant, as was homophobia: discrimination against
people who are lesbian, gay, bisexual, transgender, or queer,
those who love people of the same sex. Mom shared Dad's
passion for progressive causes, but while he fought injustice
in the courts, she was bound to us kids and had to find her
own ways to resist the status quo.

Her keen interest in social issues and politics ended up
being what kept Mom sane in those years. With a tree house
in the backyard, a basketball hoop in the driveway, and a
station wagon parked in the garage, we looked like the
quintessential upper-middle-class Dallas family. But while
other families bowled, we did politics.

While we were growing up, our dinner table was never
for eating—it was for sorting precinct lists, which is how
voters are organized into neighborhoods around the polling places where they vote. The earliest photo I have of me
walking is at age two, out on our front lawn with a yard sign
advertising the congressional campaign of Barefoot Sanders,
a progressive Democrat. Our after-school activities were as
likely to include stuffing envelopes at campaign headquarters as they were going to gymnastics or soccer practice.

As time passed and my parents' involvement in local politics expanded, our house on Lovers Lane became the local gathering place for misfits and rabble-rousers, with parties until the wee hours. It was one long continuum of liberal camaraderie, and Mom was the life of the party. It was much later that I realized those early days may have foreshadowed my mother's struggle

**Does your family do volunteer activities together? If you could choose, what volunteer activities would you like to do together?**

with drinking too much alcohol. All of their friends drank, so it never seemed out of the ordinary. Didn't everybody's parents have a few martinis before dinner?

Of course we kids were sleeping during most of those late nights. More than once, my siblings and I would wake

My first campaign: Barefoot Sanders's run for Congress. Dallas, 1958.

up for school in the morning to find some stranger snoring on the couch—the latest traveling reporter or union leader from out of town. Having grown up in that exciting environment, to me, politics never seemed like a chore; it was where the action was.

When I was twelve, we moved to Austin. If Dallas was the heart of right-wing conservatism, Austin was the motherland of the resistance. Unlike Dallas, where we never fit in, Austin was full of folks who shared our views and lifestyle. Mom threw herself into all the things she could never have done in Dallas and seemed to be having a blast.

As they had done in Dallas, my parents hung out at the Unitarian church, less for the religion than for finding a community of other liberals. The kids at church, including my oldest friend, Jill Whitten, whose family had moved to Austin from Dallas a few years earlier, had welcomed me to town, and they were up-to-date on all the political activities, especially the protests against the war in Vietnam. Kids were planning to wear black armbands to school in solidarity.

Listening to music in my bedroom, I considered whether I too might wear an armband. I was still relatively new to Austin and had spent most of my time just trying to adjust to a new school. We lived in the country, outside of town, and I didn't know how the other kids would react to my political statement. Like a lot of other seventh graders, the last thing I wanted to do was draw attention to myself. But in the end, I decided that it was a good thing to do, regardless of what my classmates might think.

Before going to bed, I dug around in Mom's sewing kit and found a piece of black felt. I methodically measured and cut it into an armband big enough that it would be impossible to miss. The next morning I attached it carefully to my sleeve with a safety pin and marched out the door, waving good-bye to my parents. As the oldest child, I had always tried to be perfect, and this felt like the most daring thing I had ever done. The armband might as well have had the word *agitator* sewn onto it.

Stepping onto the school bus, I glanced around, trying to play it cool, even though my stomach was churning. I found my friend Alison and sat with her, dodging the paper airplanes most of the other kids were tossing around. No one else wore armbands. Did they not know about the protest?

Maybe they were afraid to get in trouble. I figured that if there were going to be consequences, it would be once we got to school. Sure enough, the principal at Westlake Junior High, Tom Hestand, stopped me on my way to third period and asked that I come to his office. I had never been summoned to the principal's office before, and my heart raced as I followed him and took a seat in the chair across from his desk.

> **Have you ever taken a stand about something and worried what others might think?**

"Cecile, do your parents know what you're doing?" he asked sternly.

I thought about it, keeping my cool. "I'm pretty sure they do."

"Well," he said, "surely you won't mind, then, if I give them a call."

I shrugged and watched as he dialed the phone, then listened to it ring and ring. Finally he hung up. Mom wasn't home—perhaps one of the luckiest moments in Principal Hestand's life. Having tried and failed to get me in trouble, he had no choice but to let me go back to class.

Later that evening, when I recounted the excitement of being taken to the principal's office—escorted by the principal, no less—Mom went ballistic. "Who does Principal Hestand think he is," she fumed, "trying to intimidate you just for standing up for what you believe?" It felt like Mom and I were in a conspiracy together. The rush was exhilarating. Whether he meant to or not, Principal Hestand gets credit for helping to launch my life of activism. I've always wanted to find him and thank him for getting me started!

From then on, it was *Okay, now what can I do? Where can I make a difference?*

A few months later, inspired by the first Earth Day in 1970, I started my very first organization with some girlfriends. We named it Youth Against Pollution. We picked up trash in our neighborhood and collected aluminum cans in the lunchroom. Then I enlisted the help of my brother Dan to crush them for recycling.

My family always had lots of dogs, many of which just sort of showed up. I became obsessed with washing out all the dog food cans to recycle them. Dad found me doing it in the kitchen one day and asked me in exasperation, "Cecile, don't you know that it's pointless to wash out all those dog food cans?"

"It's for the environment!" I protested.

Dad did what he so often did when he thought an idea was harebrained: he told me exactly how he felt, in no uncertain terms. "You're not going to save the environment by washing out those goddamn dog food cans," he said, shaking his head. "Don't you know that companies are going to have to start doing this for it to make any difference?"

Dad thought I was nuts, and that wasn't the last time. Despite his idealism, he often let me know how impractical I was—and of course I was so desperate to make him proud. It took decades before I began to understand that he must have felt pride all along, even

> **Have you ever tried to do something that's different from what your parents think?**

if he sometimes had trouble expressing it. I'm sure seeking his approval helped drive me to try harder. But it also might have been my first lesson in the importance of doing what feels right and not getting too caught up in what others think—including my father. And I guess in a way we were both right. Recycling did catch on, but it had to begin somewhere. I like to think it got a jump start from teenagers washing out dog food cans.

Even in Austin, the promised land, there were problems. I was really tall, so logically I wanted to play basketball. But this was before Title IX, the federal law that now guarantees equal opportunity for girls in school activities. Back then the geniuses who determined the rules for junior high sports made us play half-court basketball. They didn't think girls could handle running up and down the full court.

And then there was football, the entire focus of our junior high and high school. I was too tall to even try out for the cheerleading squad, which outraged my mother. I opted not to take on this fight, since I would rather have died than be a part of the football scene.

Instead some friends and I fought against having to go to the weekly pep rallies—demanding a study hall for students who didn't want to cheer on the football team. At Westlake pretty much every teacher was a coach, so history and science and even sex ed were taught by folks whose primary responsibility was coaching football. As you might imagine, I was a thorn in their side.

Coach C doubled as a football coach and my eighth-grade history teacher. It was pretty obvious what his first love was, as he mainly used the blackboard for drawing football plays. When he asked us to bring in newspaper articles to discuss, I brought in one about a student who was suspended for shining his shoes with an American flag. I was outraged on the student's behalf.

"Richards!" Coach C yelled, like I was on his junior varsity team. "That kid got just what he deserved!" I never backed down from a debate with Coach C, and he definitely got me to speak up, since I disagreed with almost everything he believed.

Despite this unintended sharpening of my debate skills,

it was clear that Westlake High was a dead end for me, and after a while I was spending more time trying to figure out how to skip school and raise hell than anything else. I was a good enough student, so my parents decided to move me to St. Stephen's, a small Episcopal school. It was the first racially integrated school I'd ever attended, and it changed the direction of my life. Suddenly I had the opportunity to learn from really smart teachers alongside kids from different races and backgrounds. It felt like the world was opening up. I threw myself into acting and music and writing, all of which gave me confidence to express opinions and speak in front of others.

Though I loved my family and didn't know much beyond Texas, I couldn't shake the feeling that there had to be more.

My family in Austin, 1970: Mom, Clark, me, Ellen, Dan, and Dad, embracing the hippie culture.

Dad's mother, Eleanor Richards, planted that seed in me.

Eleanor, or Momel, grew up at a time when women were expected to stay in the kitchen, but she had seen the world. She had gone to Radcliffe College in Cambridge, Massachusetts, and had been to China and India and Africa. She helped start the League of Women Voters in Texas and fought for integration and civil rights. I loved her. More than anyone in my family, she talked about the world and politics and issues nonstop.

Momel had big plans for me. When I was still in high school, she invited me to go with her to London for a week. No one I knew had been out of the country, unless it was to go across the Texas border for Mexican food. We went to the theater, took a boat down the River Thames, and visited Windsor Castle and Buckingham Palace. When I came back from England, I told my parents they were not going to believe what was going on outside Texas.

Meanwhile, every movement of the 1960s and 1970s was coming alive, and it seemed like my parents were into them all. Mom especially threw herself into one well-intentioned hobby after another. At one point we even raised chickens in our backyard, until the fateful day that one of our many dogs got into the pen and committed the Great Chicken Massacre. ("But just think how happy that dog was!" Mom consoled my brother Dan.) Everything Mom did was larger than life, a full-scale production. But when she discovered the women's movement, she found her perfect outlet. After all, she'd spent some of her best years taking care of four kids, and she'd volunteered on many campaigns, helping to elect male friends to the Texas legislature, which is like the Congress for the state, where elected officials make laws.

I was sixteen when a young lawyer in Austin named Sarah Weddington decided to run for the state legislature. She came to Mom, asking for help. It was a golden opportunity for Mom, and she seized it. She would gather us up in the back seat of the car and take us to Sarah's headquarters, where we further refined our campaign skills, learning to make calls as part of a phone bank and to door knock to get voters to come out in support of Sarah.

Mom came up with one original idea after another for Sarah's campaign, but it was a really tough race, and I saw firsthand just how ugly it could be for a woman to run for office. This was especially true for Sarah, who had made a name for herself at the age of twenty-six arguing *Roe v. Wade* before the US Supreme Court, the case that legalized abortion (the right for women to end their pregnancies) in America. Sexism was widespread in Texas politics; one of Sarah's opponents refused to call her by name, instead referring to her as "that sweet little girl." And she even faced opposition from her own party, the Democrats.

Despite all the nastiness, Sarah won—the first woman to represent our county in the Texas House of Representatives. Her victory gave Mom the chance to finally get out of the house and go work at the capitol as Sarah's legislative assistant. This was a profound change, because up until then, it was my dad who got all the notoriety and fame. By then he was a big-deal labor and civil rights lawyer. But even we kids could tell Mom was coming into her own, and we were proud of her. After years of organizing the family, she was putting those skills to use organizing political campaigns, and she was really good at it. For the first time, we saw Mom in charge. It seemed like she knew everything.

Increasingly, as Mom was figuring out her path and my father was filling his spare time hanging out with his drinking and lawyering buddies, I was looking ahead to college. I read about Brown University in Providence, Rhode Island, where students had taken over a university building and were protesting racism and financial aid cuts. Now, that sounded like my kind of place.

But when I met with my college counselor, he told me, "I don't think you're likely to get into that school. So I've put together a list of schools that you should try instead."

Like Principal Hestand, he seemed to be trying to take me down a few notches, and I wasn't going to let him.

"Okay, well, I think I'm going to try anyway," I said. I figured out how to get the application and put together some recommendations. I was proud of myself for getting it done on my own.

In those days the college acceptance and rejection letters all arrived in mailboxes across America on April 1. When the day arrived, I could hardly breathe as I walked down the road to our mailbox. Inside was a fat letter from Brown. I tore it open and read that I had been accepted.

I was leaving Texas for a chance to see the world and make trouble.

And that's just what I did.

# Question Authority

Until the day I moved to Providence, Mom and I had never been to Rhode Island or even nearby. Still, she was certain she knew all about East Coast colleges, including what people wore.

Before leaving, we went shopping at the downtown Scarborough's department store in Austin. Mom had lots of rules where clothing was concerned. Once, when I was in fifth grade, and after endless begging, she relented and agreed to take me shopping to get something that looked more like what other girls my age wore for an upcoming slumber party. The red bell-bottom jeans with white polka dots and a robin's-egg-blue jumpsuit I picked out were my first expressions of liberation. In junior high I had perfected the art of wearing a mother-approved outfit to the breakfast table before school, then dashing downstairs, throwing on a tie-dyed T-shirt and patched bell-bottoms, and racing away on my bike before she could catch me. It was my own personal act of resistance, and it became an ongoing battle once she caught on.

The college shopping trip was her last chance to put her stamp on my appearance. She decided I needed some prim wool, mid-calf A-line skirts (won't show dirt, go anywhere), and wool turtleneck sweaters. This was a university where the students had recently occupied the administration offices, and we were coming from a state where the temperature never drops below forty degrees, but that wasn't about to stop Mom. Per usual, I had absolutely no say in the wardrobe decisions.

It was the fall of 1975. Mom's life was changing too. Not long before, the local progressive Democrats had asked my dad about running for a local office—county commissioner—but he knew it wasn't a good fit for him. He responded, "Well, why not Ann? She knows everything about political campaigns, certainly more than the rest of us." Mom recalled that there was dead silence. No one stepped in to say, "Ann, that's a wonderful idea!" or "You'd be a great choice!" She realized no one was going to come begging, not even with her success on Sarah Weddington's campaign. And so, after encouraging countless other women to run for office, Mom decided to take her own advice and give it a shot.

As I left Texas, it was clear to me that even if I returned home, nothing was ever going to be the same. By then Mom was into the women's movement with both feet. She had met lots of other activists around the fight to pass the Equal Rights Amendment, or ERA, which would have guaranteed a constitutional right to women's equality. The amendment needed Congress to pass it and at least thirty-eight states to ratify it in order for it to succeed, so women were organizing all across America.

The ERA provided the first window into my mother's and father's different attitudes when it came to so-called women's issues. Dad had spent his entire career fighting for voting rights, civil rights, and expanded opportunities for people of color to serve in office. But even he couldn't see why passing a constitutional amendment guaranteeing women's equality was necessary. He had a wife who raised the kids, took care of every single dog and cat we brought home, hosted dinner parties, and grew organic vegetables.

Dad had grown up—and was living in—a household where women threw themselves into volunteer work and didn't have careers. I realize now that for him (and so many other men of his generation), the prospect of total upheaval of home life must have seemed pretty frightening. Suddenly the tumult around women's roles and aspirations wasn't happening just on television; it was happening in our own home.

That women and men are equal might seem obvious to most people, but at the time it was highly controversial. (And of course even now we are living through a political era when men—including our president—are openly questioning women's equality.) Eventually the ERA passed in Congress but failed in the states. Out of that disappointing loss came an entire generation of women activists who would go on to pass Title IX, run for office, and keep up the effort to pass the ERA—which continues even now.

In the midst of what was starting to feel like a national identity crisis, and Mom's campaign for county commissioner, I was getting ready to start a new adventure of my own.

I'd never driven more than a couple of hundred miles with my mother, but suddenly we were off on a cross-country adventure. Both of us were taking a big leap—me finally leaving home and her running for office. In fact, she would be elected county commissioner that November. Our lives were about to change forever, but I don't remember our discussing anything more substantial than the weather during those long hours on the road.

When Mom left me on campus, I felt unbearably lost and alone. There wasn't another wool skirt in sight! All I wanted was to be cool, to be accepted. But I was the epitome of uncool and felt completely out of place. It seemed as though everyone else had been to the same summer camps and prep schools. They wore the same clothes, looking effortlessly hip, as though they hadn't given their appearance a second thought. I quickly hid my new wardrobe in the back of the dorm room closet.

Kids at Brown were smart and self-confident. For lots of them, Brown was just the continuation of high school; it seemed like pretty much everyone knew someone who knew someone.

A lottery had placed me into a small freshman seminar with Ed Beiser, who I quickly learned was one of the most revered and feared professors on campus. I was incredibly intimidated. But one day after class, he called me over to his desk. "Ms. Richards, that was a smart point you made today," he told me. "You've got something to say. I wonder, why don't you share your opinion like the other students?"

I was dumbstruck. Did he really think so?

He looked me square in the eye. "You are just as smart as any student from an East Coast prep school. Don't be afraid to stand up for what you believe." It was a rare word of encouragement from a man who believed in me more than I believed in myself.

> **Who believes in you?**

I had the chance to follow Professor Beiser's advice not long after, when the janitors on campus went on strike and suddenly this supercool, activist university became a battleground between a rich Ivy League corporation and the folks who cleaned our dorms. The administration told students the strike was uncalled for; they claimed the wages and benefits the janitors were protesting were fair. I felt caught in the middle, and never more than the day I left my dorm and saw Eddie, my freshman-year janitor, picketing with others. I called my dad and asked him what I was supposed to do. I had been taught to always side with the union. This was the kind of parental advice Dad probably always dreamed of giving. He said that in all his years of working for unions, he'd learned that the workers never got a fair shake unless they organized. He told me to always support the workers.

Some students were building a support group for the strikers, and so I dove in headfirst, finally feeling I'd found kindred spirits at Brown. We organized support for the janitors, coordinating fellow students to protest in solidarity with them. We handed out leaflets at campus events and demanded to meet with the administration.

Soon the campus librarians also organized and went on strike. One night we held a candlelight vigil. We created a V-formation of students leading up to the Rock, the primary library on campus, so anyone who wanted to get in had to walk through all of us. I guess it was easy enough to support the janitors, or at least no great inconvenience, but now students had to decide whether to cross a picket line of the library staff they depended on in order to do their research. I was disappointed as I watched people I knew cavalierly cross the line. It hurt, and I lost friendships over it.

To me, though, the choice was clear. The popular slogan of the day declared "Question Authority," and that's precisely what we were doing. At one point I called my dad and asked, "Just in case I get arrested, can you make sure you can bail me out?" He laughed, but I'm pretty sure he would have been proud if I had—though he would never have said so out loud. Eventually the university came to an agreement about wages and working conditions with the unions, and to this day the janitors and librarians at Brown have union representation.

In high school I'd organized food support for strikers at the Longhorn Machine Works in Kyle, Texas, during a bitter labor battle. I'd grown up marching with the farmworkers with my family. But Brown was the first time I'd gotten in so deep. In my classes I was learning about the American

Revolution and reading *We Shall Be All*, a book about the Industrial Workers of the World. It was dawning on me that history wasn't just something to read about in books—it was being made right in front of us, and we were a part of it.

Once you start questioning authority, it's hard to stop. I was one semester into my sophomore year and starting to wonder whether Brown and I were meant to be together. I wanted to find a place where I could figure out what I was doing in college, and more than that, what I was supposed to do with my life.

**How do you question authority?**

The second semester was rapidly approaching, so I had to make a plan. I learned of an organization in Washington, DC, working on equity in school funding for women and girls. I thought hard and decided to drop out of college and give it a try.

My parents were shocked when I called them with the news.

"What in God's name, Cecile? You are just throwing away your education," said Mom, but they knew they couldn't stop me.

I moved to Washington that winter, right after the first semester of school was over, short on street smarts and with zero experience but thrilled to be on my own. With no place to live, and long before the days of the Internet or mobile phones, I found a note tacked up at the local food market advertising for a roommate. I moved into a group house at 1927 S Street—no air-conditioning and totally bare bones.

I'd found an internship working with the Project on

the Status and Education of Women. They were fighting to implement Title IX, which required for the first time that women and men have equal opportunities in education. For one thing, Title IX said that a university that spent $50 million on football had to spend $50 million on women's sports. As a Texan, I knew how much money, time, and talent was poured into football, and the thought that the same amount now had to be spent on girls' sports was really exciting. Maybe they could even play full-court basketball! By dumb luck I had landed in the heart of feminist organizing in America. The world was starting to open up for women, and the women's movement was putting some life-changing wins on the board.

The women I worked with made policy and created opportunities for hundreds of thousands of women and girls across America. I attended congressional hearings, researched legal issues, and generally helped out while trying to learn what I could. I couldn't have known at age twenty how much the work I was doing would influence my daughters' lives. Decades later, my daughter Hannah would be a softball pitcher and soccer player, and my other daughter, Lily, would be coxswain of the boys' high school crew team, both embodying the change that was ultimately made possible under Title IX.

My time in Washington, DC, confirmed my suspicion that there were all kinds of exciting things going on outside of college, which was the reason I had left Texas in the first place. Who knew that instead of just protesting unfair laws, you could go out and change them?

By the time my internship was up that summer, I wasn't the same person I had been when I left Brown, but I knew I was going to go back. I wanted to get my degree, and I had a renewed sense of purpose. Maybe the organizing I did between classes at Brown could actually become my career, even my life. It was clear to me that my path was to take classes by day, but spend all my free time fighting for social justice.

Instead of moving back to a dorm, I moved into a group house full of artists, proto-hippies, and people who wanted to live in a shared space. We did everything together, including cook all our meals. I joyfully learned to make food for twenty-four people, and I worked at the campus coffeehouse to make extra cash.

One day a friend suggested starting a food co-op, a low-cost market that's equally owned by all the members. I thought it was a grand idea, so naturally she got me to manage it. In a co-op, you buy the food in bulk, and then all the members have to volunteer to keep it running. We started with fifty households of Brown students, and we called it the Thursday Food Co-op. Each week we'd take grocery orders from everyone. Then, on Thursday mornings, I'd get up at the crack of dawn with Henry, who ran the food co-op in town and had a truck.

We'd drive to the produce market that served all the restaurants and grocery stores in downtown Providence and pack the truck with dozens of crates of tomatoes and lettuce and whatever was in season. It required a crazy amount of coordination, especially when it came to finding students to

fill shifts dividing up oranges and artichokes, weighing pea-
nuts, and cutting cheese into one-pound chunks. Running a
food co-op was a perfect job for an organizer: people would
stop me on campus saying, "We ran out of cashews!" or
"Household 32 never picked up their order!" Food pickup
days were chaotic and wonderful and communal—like
bringing a little bit of Austin sensibility to the Ivy League.

As an equal-opportunity agitator, I didn't pass up any
chance to make a commotion. During the summer of my
junior year, the environmental movement was in its heyday,
which was how I found myself signing up for the Clamshell
Alliance along with my surfer boyfriend. The "clams," as
they were known, were a Quaker-led group fighting against
nuclear power. The big target of the moment was the
planned Seabrook nuclear plant, which was being built in
New Hampshire. The fight over Seabrook had been going
on for a few years, and this felt like a last-ditch opportunity
to raise public awareness of the danger of nuclear power and
hopefully stop the construction.

Every detail of the occupation had to be planned by con-
sensus of the whole group; that was how the Quakers rolled.
We would be camping overnight, so all of us had to agree
on all kinds of weighty issues, like whether to bring crunchy
peanut butter or smooth. Our group had to organize the
tents and gear—perfect for me, being a veteran camper. But
we had also been warned to get gas masks, since folks were
pretty sure that the police would set off tear gas against anyone who tried to break into the construction site.

A friend and I discovered an army-navy surplus store a few hours' drive away, where we picked up gas masks for the group at a bargain price, along with some industrial-grade wire cutters and utility gloves for taking down the fence at the nuclear site. I've always wondered what the army-navy store manager thought of these two college students buying equipment for what could have been a bank robbery.

It was gray and rainy when we arrived at Seabrook, and the land around the site was a wet mess as far as the eye could see—which, it turned out, wasn't very far through the small window on my gas mask.

Although there were hundreds of us—activists from all over the Northeast—the odds against us were ridiculous. We were taking on the nuclear power industry and the state police. Still, it felt satisfying. There were plenty of protests I'd participated in, where, if we ever actually stopped and thought about our chances of success, we never would have done it. Seabrook definitely fell into that category.

We made camp, then trudged through the mud over to the chain-link fence. As a Quaker group, we practiced nonviolence, but that did not apply to property. The people armed with wire cutters made their way to the front. There was a loud snip, and we let out a cheer.

We had just begun to tear down portions of the fence when suddenly the state police were on us. They ripped the gas mask off my head and confiscated it—they must have figured that was simpler than teargassing the hundreds of protesters. I was outraged—I'd bought that gas mask fair and square!

We had hoped for arrests—unlike the days of the janitors' strike, I was no longer afraid to go to jail—but the police refused to take us into custody given the limited accommodations of the Seabrook city lockup. Instead we held a makeshift march outside the capitol in Concord, New Hampshire. We were proud to have taken a stand against the plant, and it was gratifying to be part of the movement to resist nuclear power. As one of our protest signs said, "Better active now than radioactive tomorrow!"

**Have you ever tried to do something important that you knew deep down was hopeless? Why did you continue?**

Seabrook wound up being one of my less successful efforts. The plant was up and running by 1990, and is to this day one of the biggest nuclear plants in New England. I knew taking on an entire industry with my fellow "clams" wasn't going to change the course of history, but we had set out to make a statement, and that's just what we had done. It felt so much more rewarding to go out and do something about environmental policy instead of just talking about it in class.

As college was winding down, I began talking to my co-conspirators at Brown about what to do next. We were on our way to massive social change, I just knew it. We had developed our organizing skills, and now we would be set loose in the world. But to my total disbelief, most of the folks I had been in the trenches with were actually going straight! They were heading to law school, becoming psychiatrists like their parents, or going to New York to work in publishing. What about the revolution we were building? What about all the issues we had fought for and were committed to?

Right around this time I read *Living My Life*, the autobiography of the 1930s radical Emma Goldman. Goldman would travel the country, lecturing on college campuses and urging students to recognize their privilege. In no uncertain terms, she would tell them that they would not be where they were without the blood and sweat of working people who had sacrificed for them. Reading her words, I felt she was talking right to me: I was in college because my grandfather, who had owned an Iowa seed company, had put aside the money for my tuition, and I wanted to pay back the opportunity I'd been given.

Being a troublemaker wasn't exactly a career, and nobody's folks paid for four years at Brown University to have their child choose that path. I had no idea how I'd make a living, but by now I'd seen enough people fighting for social good that I knew it was the life for me. Applying to law school like my dad was not in the cards; sitting in more classrooms was near the bottom of the list of ways I wanted to spend my time. I decided that my next move would be to get an organizing job with a union, though I soon learned that organizing jobs were few and far between. With help from my dad, I sent letter after letter to a slew of unions. They began, "I am interested in any openings you have for union organizers, anywhere in the country. I can start immediately and I speak Spanish."

As I watched my friends pack up and move to new

places for new jobs or, more often, move back to where they came from, I felt the familiar pangs of being an outsider who just couldn't take the conventional route. I was restless and eager for my next adventure. Brown had actually prepared me for the career I wanted: I may have majored in history, but I minored in agitating. I learned something from each thing I did—organizing with the janitors, supporting the librarians, protesting in Seabrook, even running the campus coffeehouse and food co-op. My time in college taught me a lesson I have carried through my life: don't sit around and wait for the perfect opportunity to come along—find something and *make* it an opportunity.

# 3

# It's Not the Work,
# It's Who You Work With

Imet Kirk Adams on Memorial Day in 1981, when he walked into the United Labor Union (ULU) offices in downtown New Orleans. The first thing I noticed was his outfit: neatly creased khaki pants, button-down shirt, lace-up brown shoes. I took one look at him and thought, *Great-looking guy, nice smile. He'll last a week.* Kirk remembers that I had on a leotard top, a jeans skirt, and flats, which had all been bought at a secondhand clothing store, my go-to in those days. The way he tells it, he fell in love at first sight.

I'd been at the ULU for about a year by then. It was a scrappy upstart dedicated to organizing low-wage workers for better pay and working conditions. In New Orleans that meant hotel workers. By the time Kirk showed up, I'd seen many would-be organizers come through town, but few stuck it out. I was in charge of newcomers, so I gave him a list of hotel workers to visit and put him on a bus to the

Desire housing projects, where a lot of the workers lived.

I didn't expect to see him again. Not only did he come back, but he'd actually been hugely successful in getting folks to think about starting a union, after they figured out he wasn't a missionary or an insurance collector. As it turned out, Kirk knew what it was like for working-class families because he had come from one himself in Massachusetts: his mom had worked the midnight shift at the post office, and his father was a milkman. Underneath that button-down shirt, he was a troublemaker at heart.

---

**Have you ever wrongly judged someone at first glance?**

---

By then I was renting an apartment in Mid-City from a wild artist who made life-size stuffed puppets. They were scattered all over the apartment, along with about seventy house plants that, in exchange for cheap rent, I was supposed to keep alive. As a gritty little organizing team, we at ULU were constantly putting up traveling staff and anyone we could convince to join our merry band. That's how Kirk ended up staying at my house when he first arrived in town. He didn't know anyone, so I said he could sleep on my living room couch until he found a place.

If union organizing is a foreign concept to you, here's the lowdown: Unions are one of the main ways workers can fight for good wages and benefits. If you're looking for a job but aren't in a union, you have to take whatever the company offers—for pay and for the hours you'll have to work. If you're in a union, you are protected, because all the workers band together and demand good working conditions and decent pay. Employers have a whole lot of power on their side, and the best way for workers to bargain with them is if they all stand together.

Back when Emma Goldman was agitating, men, women, and children were expected to work fourteen or more hours a day, every day, in dangerous factories or mines, for barely enough money to afford a decent meal and rent. And if you got sick or hurt on the job, you were on your own. For the most part, it's not like that anymore. But having strong unions doesn't just make things better for union members: if your family enjoys affordable health care and your parents an eight-hour workday with weekends off, thank the labor movement in America, which fought for those rights that we now take for granted.

To win a union campaign—that is, the right of workers at a particular company to form a union—two things usually have to happen. First, employees show their interest by signing a union card or petition, which means they want to unionize. Then, often, a government-run secret-ballot election is held to see if their coworkers feel the same way, with a representative of the federal National Labor Relations Board coming out to monitor the vote. If a majority of workers vote for the union, the employer has to bargain with the employees as one big group in order to reach a labor contract, spelling out wages, hours, and working conditions. This is called collective bargaining, because the employer has to negotiate with the workers as a block, rather than playing one worker off another.

That's union organizing in theory. In practice it's an

uphill battle and frequently risky for the workers who are willing to stick out their necks to fight for a decent wage. During the process, employees are often harassed or fired, or they quit due to the pressure. It can be incredibly hard to win a union election, and even harder to get someone's job back when he or she is illegally fired. It might take years for an employee to win his or her case, by which time the union campaign is usually long over. That's especially true for workers earning the minimum wage, the wage set by the government as the lowest that an employer can legally pay. Usually, minimum-wage work still means that the people earning it will live in poverty.

As organizers, our job was to go to workplaces—from hotels to hospitals—and talk with folks about forming a union. As you might expect, employers don't exactly roll out the red carpet when they see an organizer coming, so we wound up spending most of our time waiting around to talk to employees when they got off work.

At my first job I hung around outside a garment factory in Texas and made conversation with the primarily Latina workers either on lunch break or after the workday ended. It's crazy now to think of grown women, most of them supporting kids and sometimes their own parents as well, talking to me about starting a union. What did a white kid fresh out of college know about the world? It was as humbling as it was eye-opening. Many of these women had already risked so much to come to the United States. They knew they were not being treated fairly on the job. Whatever apprehension they felt about talking to me was outweighed by their desire

to make something better for themselves and, more important, for their kids. They didn't want their daughters to end
up sewing jeans for $3.35 an hour.

Back when Mom was starting to get into politics, she
often reminded me, "People don't do things for *your*
reasons—they do things for *their* reasons." What I learned
in that first year, sitting in trailers in rural Texas or at the local
church or coffee shop, was that the women I met would do
just about anything to improve their lives, including talking
to me about banding together with their fellow workers.

On my first day at the ULU, I was hanging around outside the Warwick Hotel in downtown New Orleans when I
spotted a young woman dressed in a housekeeping uniform.
She looked determined, like her shift had just ended and
she was out of there—just the kind of person I was hoping
to talk to. As she headed toward the bus stop, I intercepted
her and introduced myself. "I've heard that the wages and
working conditions at the Warwick are pretty tough, and
I wanted to see if we can do something about it," I said.
Glancing over her shoulder to make sure no one from the
hotel was watching, she asked for my phone number. "I'll
call you later," she promised, running for her bus.

In my short career as an organizer, I'd had plenty of similar conversations that never actually resulted in the promised call. So I was surprised when the phone rang later that
day, and it was the young woman. She told me that working
in the hotel was a horror. Hotels were notorious for putting white male employees in the cushy "front of the house"
jobs, staffing the front desk or working as a bellman, where

they got tips. Like most African American women in the service industry, this woman was stuck in housekeeping, working long hours for terrible pay. When rooms were full, she had to pull double shifts. But in the slow season, she didn't work enough to make ends meet—that is, her wages weren't enough to feed, clothe, and house her family. There were no guarantees of a weekly paycheck, and when she did work, she was cleaning fourteen rooms a day.

After that initial call, we started getting together after work. She said she had friends who wanted to talk too. Soon we were meeting with other housekeepers, busboys, janitors, and cooks from the hotel—all of whom were working for low pay with no hope of advancement. They weren't naive; they knew just talking to us could cost them their jobs, but that was a chance they were willing to take. Sure enough, management started firing and harassing people right and left.

One of the many wise workers I met was Charles Husband, a maintenance employee at the Warwick and a natural philosopher. The young guys at work looked up to him, and though he knew our odds of successfully forming a union were almost nonexistent, he believed that standing up for himself and his coworkers was worth taking the chance. Charles taught me a fundamental truth about organizing: despite the terrible wages and working conditions, what mattered most to the workers was

**Are there problems you feel so passionately about that you are willing to take a risk to solve them? What are those problems?**

gaining respect from their boss. And if they lost their job in the process, as Charles would say, "I was looking for a job when I got this one." In other words, there was always going to be more work, but nothing was going to change unless someone was willing to stand up and fight back.

There was no such thing as a time clock or a regular schedule; we followed the schedules of the service workers. I witnessed firsthand the enormous challenges they faced both at work and in their personal lives. The women in particular weren't just figuring out how to make it until payday. They were the ones tasked with finding someone to take their kids when they got called in at the last minute or looking for a ride to get their mom to church on Sunday. Their responsibilities didn't end when they left their job at the end of the day; they just changed locations.

> **Who watches young kids when their parents are at work? What if a family can't afford to pay a sitter or doesn't have relatives nearby who can help take care of the kids?**

For all the time and effort we put in, we were hardly what you would call successful. In between organizing twelve hours a day, our team did whatever we could think of to keep the union afloat.

We ate, slept, and breathed the union. We fund-raised on street corners all around New Orleans—it was really more like organized begging—and canvassed door to door, which was more respectable but even more uncomfortable. (Nothing is quite so humiliating as asking for a contribution and having the door slammed in your face.) I learned quickly that I would never starve, though some days we came a little too close for comfort.

We all found ourselves doing things we might not have pictured. Kirk once stood on a street corner at Claiborne and Carrollton Avenues in New Orleans, looking so clean-cut, shaking a can to raise money for the union. A guy drove up and rolled down his window at the intersection: it was one of Kirk's classmates from Wesleyan University. Kirk said hi and explained to his surprised classmate what he was doing. At least the guy gave him a dollar—our goal was "No contribution that clinked." It was a little embarrassing for Kirk, but he took it in stride. Three months later Kirk went back to Boston to help out on a home-care organizing campaign for the union. They too were trying to make ends meet, and he was shaking a can on Massachusetts Avenue when the same guy pulled up again. Kirk explained sheepishly that he was an expert at can shaking, so he had gone national.

Somewhere along the way Kirk and I went from roommates to friends and ended up dating. Both our families supported our work unconditionally, even if they were slightly mystified by the lives we'd chosen for ourselves. As Kirk's dad would say to him, shaking his head: "I can't believe they pay you to make trouble."

After two years in New Orleans—one year for Kirk—we were ready for a change. For all our enthusiasm, our team's organizing efforts weren't succeeding. One day Gerry Shea, a big shot with the Service Employees Union, came through

New Orleans. They were going to try to organize a union for workers at the largest for-profit nursing-home chain in the country. The chain, Beverly Enterprises, had made a fortune buying up nursing homes and cutting wages to the bone—and one of the crown jewels was Texas. Gerry hired both of us. So not long afterward Kirk and I loaded up our car with everything we owned. (Well, almost everything. We had to leave the toaster oven behind; we just didn't have the space.) With that, we headed to Houston.

From the moment we started our new jobs we were on the road, traveling all over East Texas. It seemed like every small town had a Beverly nursing home, and we set out to unionize them all. The women we organized were doing the Lord's work taking care of the elderly, but making less than four dollars an hour, which was only slightly more than minimum wage.

Most of the places we organized were in deep East Texas, which was as segregated a world as I'd ever seen. After a few months Kirk and I migrated to Tyler, where there were many more women to organize. We moved into a small red-brick house, where we could live in the back and hold union meetings in the front. The house was on Houston Street, in the middle of town, pretty much right on the racial divide between north and south Tyler. The day we arrived, our neighbors came over to bring us some fresh-cut Tyler roses in a mason jar.

"We're so glad you moved in," they said, "because before you, there was a Negro family living here." My jaw dropped; I was horrified by the racism.

Much to our neighbors' dismay, our house became the central gathering spot for African American nursing-home workers. Women pulled up in their run-down Chevrolets and parked in the front yard, before and after their shifts, for union meetings in our living room.

There wasn't much to do in Tyler, so we made our own fun. It was where I reinvented the Richards family tradition of "all-come" dinner parties—everyone was invited.

Most important, Tyler was where I learned that, even in the midst of soul-crushing poverty, people could celebrate and love life. East Texas was a tough place to live—especially if you were African American, and a woman to boot. When we won a union election, it was time to rent a room at the Ramada Inn, get somebody's son to DJ, and have a blast. Even though the days were hard, some of our very best times were celebrating with the amazing women employee leaders of East Texas.

The years we spent in East Texas reminded me of a question the longtime farmworker organizer Marshall Ganz had posed years earlier: What's the definition of a leader? His answer: Someone who has followers. The women we organized with didn't have money or fame or political influence, but everybody looked up to them. Jeril was raising her daughters on her minimum-wage salary from the nursing home in Bryan, and her apartment was the center of her community. Vicki in Texas City was constantly taking second jobs so she could finally buy a home of her own. She never missed a day's work, and she was committed to her patients. And Georgia Landry in Beaumont was everyone's grandmother, working the overnight shift and encouraging the younger new employees to stick with the job. These were women who had earned the respect of their coworkers and, more often than not, the unspoken admiration of their employers.

The organizing campaigns were ugly, and they were tough. Folks were threatened and fired, but they persevered. We held elections in town after town and had the best winning streak in the union.

> **Can you think of someone unexpected who is a leader but not famous? Why do you admire this person?**

Beverly Enterprises was as cheap as dirt, and the new union contracts they made with workers provided barely more than what the workers were earning before we started. But the women wanted respect and recognition for the work they did, and organizing a union accomplished that. Their bosses had to sit across the table from them as equals and talk about wages and working conditions, and that had never happened before.

After we'd been in Texas for a while, Kirk and I decided to get married at my mom's house in Austin. It was not a traditional wedding in anyone's book, with my off-the-rack dress and my refusal to be "given away" by my dad. Really, our wedding was more of a continuation of our organizing life. So as soon as the "I dos" were finished, we raced to Beaumont in Southeast Texas to prepare for the biggest nursing-home strike in Texas history. A few years earlier the

Our wedding.

women at the Schlesinger nursing home had organized and bargained a union contract with the best wages in the state. But when it came time to renegotiate a new contract, the employer decided to try to break the union and force the women to go out on strike or work for lower wages. It was against the law, but employers got away with it all the time.

We decided there was no option but to strike.

We didn't make this decision lightly. Strikers take a huge risk when they stop work. They lose pay for the days they strike, and these were workers who didn't have any wiggle room in their incomes. They were barely making enough money to live, let alone stash away savings to get them through a long work stoppage. Strikers also risk losing their jobs if the company decides it can walk away from the negotiations and hire new workers.

We threw everything we had at the Schlesinger nursing-home owners, but they wouldn't budge, and we lost the strike. The company had hired replacement workers in order to keep the nursing home open. Our women stayed out on strike, but once employers break the union, they get to decide who they're going to bring back. Some women got their jobs back, but others did not. Even if we had won, the women we were organizing were never going to get rich or even climb out of poverty. At its core the campaign had been a fight for dignity—a way for the women to finally have their boss treat them as equals, to sit down and bargain with them. Now they were back at square one. I learned a very tough lesson that my dad had admonished me about before: never go out on strike unless you have a plan to get back in.

In a low moment I wondered whether it would have been better not to have fought at all. But while I didn't know what the outcome would be when we started, I knew for certain what it would have been if we'd never even tried. That is as true today as it was in Beaumont.

After we had run union elections in pretty much every

Beverly nursing home in East Texas, the union approached us about moving to Los Angeles, where they needed more organizing talent. By this point we were used to moving every couple of years, so we packed up the car and moved to L.A. Kirk was hired to organize seventy-two thousand home-care workers, something no one had ever done before. And I became part of the "Justice for Janitors" campaign, with the goal of unionizing the immigrant workers who cleaned the high-rise office buildings downtown.

The idea of the janitors' campaign was pretty simple: we needed to get the attention of the downtown building owners and shame them into granting better wages and working conditions to the cleaning crews. There were dozens of non-union buildings housing the most prestigious banks and law firms in town.

The janitors worked at night, usually long after all the office workers had gone home, so we would meet them outside at the food trucks at ten p.m., on their dinner break. We would flyer the building lobbies during the day with pictures of the janitors and their kids—to let company employees see that actual people with lives and families kept their offices clean and tidy late into the night. We marched through banks and law firms during the lunch hour, carrying mops and brooms and banging on enormous drums.

At this point our first daughter, Lily, had arrived, so she was raised from the start protesting on the picket line. I'd show up at night at the buildings with her in a backpack; she was at more union meetings before she could walk than most people in their entire lives. While Kirk and I ran our organizing campaigns, she would roll around the office in a baby walker, where I or another staffer could keep an eye on her.

The arrival of our Lily was lifesaving. Until then we were round-the-clock activists and organizers. We didn't even have a goldfish or a guinea pig. We barely owned a potted plant. For the first time we had to think about something other than a union meeting or staying at the office until the wee hours of the morning.

I left Lily at day care on the day we decided to escalate our union campaign, and it's a good thing I didn't bring her with me. After one of many building sit-ins, now we just had to tip it over the edge—stay put until we got arrested. And that's just what happened. After sitting in the city lockup for a few hours, arrested for disturbing the peace, we were released. I never forgot the humiliation of being fingerprinted and having a mug shot taken. Nothing about jail is glamorous.

We succeeded in letting the building owners know we were serious—and more important, we shone a light on the injustice of the wages and working conditions of the downtown janitors. There were many more chapters and arrests to come, but ultimately the Justice for Janitors campaign in Los Angeles was a success in getting union contracts downtown and eventually all across the city.

Whenever I asked the janitors about the risks involved, they would tell me what they had already sacrificed to come to the United States. Most were from Central America and had traveled by land hundreds of miles, paying smugglers to sneak them across the border. Many had left their parents, children, or spouses behind. They did it because only in America could they scrape together a better life for themselves and their kids. Despite the shamefully low pay, many counted on their minimum-wage jobs to send money back to family in the countries they came from. More than any folks I've ever worked with, they understood that life is what you make of it, and they were determined to take every opportunity they had to make something better. Now I never work in a building without knowing the janitors. In most cities they are truly the invisible ones, who work long after most people have gone home and do work that no one else would do. I always remember to thank them and make sure they are earning a living wage.

Kirk and I were on a high—our work was making a difference; we were fighting for real equity instead of just fighting for a nickel an hour more. Lily was two years old, and we were settled into our neighborhood in Venice, California, living right near the beach. Our whole life was the fight for respect and justice for the most overworked and underpaid folks in the city. We loved it.

But life happens when you're making other plans. In 1989, my mother called to say she needed us back in Texas, so we were soon packing up our California memories to head back home.

Kirk and me as union organizers, saying good-bye to janitors, health care workers, and friends in Los Angeles as we moved back to Austin.

# 4

## Going for Broke in Texas

**W**e want Ann!" the crowd chanted in Atlanta, followed by raucous applause. I looked out from the gigantic, ocean-liner-size stage where I sat alongside my brothers, Clark and Dan, and my sister, Ellen, taking in the scene. It was classic political convention-style pandemonium: folks were throwing beach balls, wearing crazy hats, and blowing horns. In a few days Michael Dukakis would accept the 1988 Democratic nomination for president from this very stage. But right now the entire convention was focused on the woman of the hour, my mom.

True to form, from the moment she had gotten the call inviting her to deliver the keynote speech at the Democratic National Convention, Mom had approached the task with military precision, right down to the eye-catching blue dress she knew would look just right on television. We had spent the days before holed up in her hotel room as she worked on her speech. It was both thrilling and nerve-racking.

Everyone on her team was suggesting lines, making edits, crossing things out, and making notes in the margins. We went through draft after draft and, as always, finished at the last possible second.

Finally the moment had arrived. I sat onstage, perched on the edge of my chair, waiting for Mom to appear. I caught sight of Kirk and Lily in the audience. Lily, who was a year and a half old, was sitting on Kirk's lap, and I thought how wonderful it was that Mom's granddaughter was getting to see this in person.

This was not Mom's first time on the national stage, but it was the most significant. When the lights dimmed, a hush fell over the crowd. People settled in to listen.

"Twelve years ago, Barbara Jordan, another Texas woman, made the keynote address to this convention," she began. "And two women in 160 years is about par for the course." The crowd erupted in laughter and applause. "But if you give us a chance, we can perform." And then, in a reference to the iconic dance partners from the old movies, she went on. "After all, Ginger Rogers did everything that Fred Astaire did. She just did it backwards and in high heels!" The speech was perfect, better than anyone could have hoped. Mom was landing every line with the audience, and they were captivated.

We were all beaming with pride by the time Mom got to the closing section. Turning sentimental, she said, "I'm a grandmother now. And I have one nearly perfect granddaughter named Lily. And when I hold that grandbaby, I feel the continuity of life that unites us, that binds generation to generation, that ties us with each other. . . . And as I look at Lily, I know that it is within families that we learn both the need to respect individual human dignity and to work together for our common good. Within our families, within our nation, it is the same." I looked out into the audience again. Kirk, who has never been a crier, had tears in his eyes. He was bouncing Lily up and down, knowing she was too young to understand why her grandmother was up on the stage in the first place.

Someone had brought Mom's parents to their local TV station in Waco, and they streamed in live to talk with Mom after the speech. The news announcer turned to Poppy, my grandfather, and said, "Well, Mr. Willis, when you told your daughter that she could do anything she wanted to do if she just worked hard enough, did you ever dream that she would be doing something like this?" Poppy laughed and said, "Why, hell, I didn't even know there *was* a this!"

Dukakis went on to a crushing defeat, but the speech made Mom a household name. Women everywhere wrote letters, asking her to run for governor of Texas, or better yet, president of the United States. Her whole world was opening up, and nothing would ever be the same.

The 1980s had brought enormous changes for Mom, and the most life-changing of these was that she had gotten sober— through treatment and therapy, she stopped drinking alcohol years before her speech at the convention.

In those days there was no easy way to publicly declare your addiction and go for treatment. It wasn't something people talked about, let alone did. I'm not sure who finally decided to break that unspoken code, but some of her friends consulted with a couple who specialized in interventions—a miserable process where loved ones confront the addict at a group meeting to persuade him or her to get help.

As with so many unpleasant things in life, the details of that day are hazy, except for this: it was horrible. I have never been good at keeping secrets, and it felt awful to plot this whole event behind Mom's back. As the oldest child, then in my early twenties, I was in on it, along with Dad and many of Mom's good friends. We gathered in someone's living room, though I cannot remember whose, and she arrived under some other pretense. We sat down in a circle of chairs, and Mom had to sit and listen to each of us tell how her drinking had affected us. "I was scared to get into the car with you when you were drinking," I told her, "and scared for the other kids too." That was all I could get out, but it was enough.

She heard so many hard and heartbreaking statements that day that she left for treatment in Minneapolis—she called it "drunk school"—the same afternoon. Later we spent a week with her to do family therapy. It was a sad time for everyone, especially Mom. I know how terrible it must have been and how ashamed she felt. But she took on therapy like everything else she'd ever done, full-on, and she never had another drink in her life.

When Mom went away for treatment, she predicted that it would be the end of her marriage. She was right: she was sober for less than six months when Dad moved out, and though she saw it coming, she was crushed.

At the time, I was working in Texas at my first union organizing job. Mom wanted companionship more than anything else as she was beginning the slow adjustment to living on her own for the first time, so we decided I'd move in with her. It was an awkward transfer of roles: she was staying at home in the evenings, and I was going out with friends, after making sure she had dinner and was going to be okay for the night.

It was a temporary arrangement, and I was anxious to get on with my life. As for Mom, she eventually got used to living alone, and once Mom came into her own, she wasn't about to go back. She felt free.

In 1982, after a tough election, she was elected treasurer of the state of Texas, becoming the first woman to hold state-wide office in Texas in more than fifty years. To most of the men who made up the Democratic Party establishment, the job seemed like appropriate women's work: nonthreatening, out of sight, kind of like keeping track of the family budget.

Her male counterparts in the Texas Democratic Party saw her as a colorful addition to the statewide team, but they didn't think of her as their competition, and certainly not as their leader. But after her star turn at the Democratic National Convention, and eight years sober, she was starting to think seriously about taking on what was certain to be an even more grueling campaign for governor. First she would have to win a primary to be the Democratic Party nominee, and only then could she vie for the governorship against whoever the Republicans nominated. She gave us fair warning that if she decided to run, she'd need our help.

When my phone rang a few months after the convention, I was at home in California, working, raising a toddler, and about as far removed from Texas politics as you can get. I wasn't ready for what she was about to ask.

"Cecile, I'm gonna do it," she said, cutting right to the chase. I took a deep breath.

"The women are on fire," she continued. "But I'm going to have a tough Democratic primary. Really tough. They are going to say I'm a drug addict and hassle me about being divorced. But if I don't do it, I will always wonder, what if? I just can't live with that."

As independent as Mom was, she had the same human frailties that we all do. After my parents' marriage unraveled, Mom had come to lean on her kids for her emotional support. My mother was a very complicated person, and although she was enormously competent and driven, she was also unsure of herself. She was always struggling to overcome the insecurities of her upbringing, trying to prove she was just as smart as the other kids. On top of that, she was trying to succeed in a political environment that was, at its roots, hostile to women.

**Is there something you feel you need to try? What is it?**

For her to be as fearless and unflappable as she was in public, she was counting on us—her kids—to be there for her during what promised to be her most daunting challenge yet, both in the Democratic primary and in the general election. Leave it to Kirk to put everything in perspective.

"If your mom needs us, we have to go back home," he said. I loved him for that.

It was never a question of *if* we would go, but the decision came with regrets. Kirk and I both felt loyalty toward our union organizing teams and worried we were letting them down. At the same time, as I packed to move to Texas, I thought about how improbable and extraordinary this was—that someone who had spent so much of her life as a housewife and had only recently gotten into politics not only wanted to be governor but actually thought she could win.

Of course, it was not lost on me that men take these chances all the time. They say, "I work for an advertising firm and have never been in public office, but I'm going to run for Congress." Women, on the other hand, say, "I was thinking about applying for that job, but I haven't finished my PhD yet."

My mother decided she wasn't going to wait until she had the perfect résumé, and she certainly wasn't going to wait until she was guaranteed success. Every political race she'd gotten into, it was because she knew that she was qualified and could do a better job than the incumbent, even if she was the only one who thought so.

For Kirk, Lily, and me, our family life became consumed by Mom's campaign. Practically overnight, the dumpy campaign headquarters became our home away from home. We never even unpacked all our boxes at the house we rented in Texas, and we never set foot in the backyard. Lily grew up at the campaign office, surrounded by a clan of staff and volunteers. Legions of folks helped raise her, and after that she never met a stranger.

Lily was two and a half. Our routine was to drop her off at day care the moment it opened and pick her up a minute before it closed (on a good day). Afterward we'd bring her back to the office for pizza while we spent the evening making phone calls to potential volunteers and county coordinators. Watching

**Who are some of the special non-family members in your life?**

her pretend to make urgent phone calls or play with the autopen machine called to mind my own young days parading on the lawn for Barefoot Sanders.

These may not have been ideal circumstances for other young families, but we were in our element. It was the ultimate organizing challenge; we knew the only way we could win the election was to build a grassroots operation in every part of the state. Texas has 254 counties, and our first priority was finding a coordinator for each of them, a herculean task.

Mom was an upstart candidate, and the people who ran her campaign were a combination of family and friends, plus talented women and political types who were intrigued by the idea of her running. When we weren't in the campaign office, we were zigzagging all over the state—which is geographically bigger than France.

Our car was like a mobile campaign unit, jammed with stickers and yard signs. On many days, early in the morning, I'd throw Lily, still in her pajamas, in the back seat and we'd

The Ann Richards campaign for governor, featuring Lily, who traveled nearly as many miles as the candidate.

hit the road, stopping to change at the local Dairy Queen. The definition of dressing up was grabbing a new pair of panty hose in "suntan" color at the 7-Eleven on the way to a speech, and a good meal was a fish sandwich with jalapeños at Whataburger.

There was no crowd too small to hand out "Ann Richards for Governor" cards. A lot of people had voted for Mom for treasurer, but they didn't know much about her. Our goal was to defang this wild idea of electing a progressive woman and to let them know that Mom was just like them. It was exciting to meet and talk with voters one on one—retail politics was as good as it got.

Best of all were the women I met along the way, women

who had been waiting for a chance like this all their lives. Women had been behind the scenes, running Democratic campaigns across the state, for as long as anyone could remember—making the calls, dividing up the block-walk lists to knock on doors, organizing the fund-raisers and chili suppers, like we always had done in our dining room growing up. Now they were doing it all for a woman, and that was a great big deal.

Everywhere I went, women my mother's age and often with her same hairdo would grab me by the arm, their eyes shining, and say, "I never thought I'd see the day!" Mom said that being a woman running for governor was like being a three-headed dog at the carnival: she was a novelty, so we got a crowd pretty much wherever we went.

The worst part of campaigning was dealing with the negative press, the rumors and personal attacks on Mom. When the news started off with "Today Ann Richards was accused of . . ." I'd turn off the TV. My job was to be the most enthusiastic warrior I could be, and that often required fielding questions from reporters that were based on half-truths and rumors. I've found that you have to decide what it is that makes you a good organizer, and what saps your strength and energy. For me, television news has always been the latter.

**What people or activities give you strength? What brings you down?**

It's easy to get caught up in the press and assume everyone else is as well, but I discovered that in most towns, people were busy just living their lives. In those places we could make a big impact just by meeting people and listening to their concerns. There's no better way to refute false attacks than to have a conversation with people and tell them what you know to be the truth.

Not everyone was a fan—witness the homecoming parade at Baylor University in Waco, where Mom had gone to college. My brother Dan had decked out his '57 Ford pickup with bunting on the sides and hay bales in the back. We climbed up into the truck. Lily sat on the hay, the center of it all, dressed in a darling red, white, and blue dress, and threw candy to the parade-goers. She had become a bit of a campaign mascot—whether she was riding on a float for a Cinco de Mayo parade in Laredo or handing out Ann Richards campaign materials at the annual Luling Watermelon Thump. She had learned early on to look someone in the eye and shake their hand, and people were charmed by her. But even Lily's winning personality wasn't always enough. We got a few scowls in the homecoming procession—it was conservative territory, after all, so we weren't expecting a welcoming committee. But it was too much when an older gentleman, dressed in a checkered shirt and jeans, stepped up and shot the middle finger at my toddler. *Welcome to hard-knuckle politics,* I thought.

But we persevered, and by the skin of our teeth we got through the primary. The grassroots organizing paid off, and the network of volunteers and supporters we built across the state gave us the edge. It was a campaign that radiated intensity and excitement. But of course it was Mom who clinched it. What people remembered when it was time to vote wasn't so much policy or a position statement; it was how Mom had made them feel. She wasn't afraid to be who she was, warts and all.

The general election meant facing Republican candidate Clayton Williams, a Texas oilman and classic sexist pig. Williams had never held public office, and he loved to make crude comments about women. He even "joked" that women should just try to enjoy rape—the crime of forcing women to have sex against their will. He was awful. Every chance he got, he'd try to physically intimidate Mom and put her off her game by looming over her or pointing his finger right into her face. My brother once asked how she managed to stay calm when dealing with Williams. "You know," she said, "my blood pressure drops. I go into cool mode. Here he is, another guy who lives a privileged life and doesn't give a damn about women. Now I get to expose that to the world. He doesn't get under my skin any more than the rest of the people I've dealt with all my life."

As the campaign went on, the days got longer and the pace picked up. With Lily in tow, I just kept campaigning from the Rio Grande border in the west to Texarkana in the east, speaking at union meetings and to teachers, reporters, and students. In the middle of it all, I discovered I was pregnant—with twins! But I kept going, though I was soon large as a barge.

The campaign went on through the summer and fall, with polls routinely showing us twenty points behind. Then one night Mom took the stage for a debate with Williams.

Ann Richards versus Clayton Williams: He was a classic good old boy who wanted to put women in their place. It didn't work.

She turned in a rock-solid performance—it was clear to all in attendance that she had won. Afterward she walked up to him and held out her hand; he looked her in the eye, turned on his heel, and walked away. Mom tried to laugh it off, saying to the person next to her, "Well, that wasn't very sportsmanlike." Ironically, after everything else he had done and said, *that* was the moment when some people began to question whether he had the temperament to be governor.

On Election Day, Mom stuck to her usual good-luck rituals: she took Lily for a walk around Town Lake in the morning, then got together with her friends for a game of bridge. Her parents came up from Waco and joined us at campaign headquarters, where they sat watching the chaos, a little wide-eyed.

At regular intervals throughout the day—nine a.m., noon, and three p.m.—calls came into the office with precinct reports, letting us know how many people had walked into their local polling place to cast a ballot. By going door to door all over the state, we had a good sense of how many voters we needed to come out at every single voting site. If numbers were low, we'd send out more folks to knock on doors and get people to the polls. If numbers were high, we'd send our organizers somewhere else. It was all a question of turnout. And our voters turned out—Mom won the race!

It was truly an organizers' victory. We had beaten the odds and elected a divorced, recovering alcoholic, feminist, progressive woman to be governor of Texas. In the end it was the determination of our volunteers that pulled us over the line. We never had a poll showing that we could win—never—and had the election taken place two days earlier or two days later, we probably wouldn't have. Still, we always believed it was possible.

Over the years plenty of folks have asked me if there are lessons to be learned from Mom's race. Aside from never putting your toddler in the middle of a college homecoming parade, I can think of a few big ones.

A woman's place is in the dome!

First, you can't win unless you compete. Campaigning teaches you about winning and losing and, probably most important, that you never get ahead unless you try. For all the people who told Mom she'd never win, she knew that the one way to guarantee that outcome was not to run in the first place. Lily still says it was Mom's first campaign that taught her anything is possible if you're willing to step up and give it a shot.

Second, politics at its best is about a lot more than expensive TV ads and polling. It is a contest of wills between folks who are satisfied with how things are and those who are passionate about what could be better. In our case it was a battle between the mostly white, male political establishment desperate to hang on to power, and those who wanted to widen the circle of opportunity for all Texans.

We had built a progressive grassroots army, and they knew that it was their work—every door they had knocked on, every phone call they had made—that put Mom in the governor's mansion.

Four years later, election night was a very different scene. Mom lost reelection to George W. Bush—yes, the same man who, a few years later, would become the forty-third president of the United States.

The election was a brutal loss. Mom's administration had brought a lot of changes—she had appointed people from diverse backgrounds who hadn't before had the opportunity to serve and she had vetoed a bill that would allow people to carry around concealed handguns. Beyond the pain and hurt I felt on a personal level, it was recognition that the state I loved was not the progressive home I thought we were building.

I'd had inklings of this during the campaign. A few weeks before the election, I was sent to hand out Ann Richards material at a plant gate in Beaumont, a place I knew well, since it was the scene of the Schlesinger nursing-home strike years earlier.

What I heard that day, as I stood outside the gates, was frightening. Grown men in hard hats with union stickers on their lunch pails cursed and snarled at me. "There is no way I'm going to vote for Ann Richards or any other left-winger who wants to take away my guns!" Or a variation: "She's a baby-killer." It was as if they were reading from a script—and a familiar one at that.

We'd heard this kind of rhetoric from our opponents plenty of times before. But from these union guys? They were our people! They were the same folks who had carried her to victory four years earlier, and by any measure Mom had done right by working people through her policies as governor. What was going on?

As Mom's loss set in, I just couldn't stop thinking about this experience in Beaumont. Something was happening, and it was about more than Mom's campaign. I had been hearing of a newly formed group called the Christian Coalition, organizing through churches, using divisive and hurtful language and rhetoric to boost turnout for right-wing candidates in the elections. Despite the name, the Christian Coalition was not a religious organization. It was a political organization, designed to elect candidates and build political power. Across the country they had quietly launched a targeted culture war to demonize politicians who supported women's rights and gun safety. They also targeted candidates who supported the rights of people in the LGBTQ community—that is, people who are lesbian, gay, bisexual, transgender, or queer.

**Can you think of organizations or people or products that "brand" themselves as one thing, when really they behave in a different way?**

Up to that point the business community—people who owned factories or businesses—had led Republicans in Texas and pretty much everywhere else. Their political priorities were fairly straightforward most of the time: keep taxes low and reduce regulation (oversight by government officials) of their businesses. But in 1994, the year Mom lost, the Republican Party took a hard right turn, which was reflected in my experience in Beaumont. But this was bigger than Mom. In fact, it was bigger than any of us.

As I weighed what to do next, I thought of a question a reporter had asked Mom after she lost the election: "What would you have done differently if you knew you were going to be a one-term governor?" She had just grinned and answered, "Oh, I probably would have raised more hell." I decided it was time for me to start raising some hell of my own.

# 5

## Don't Wait for Instructions

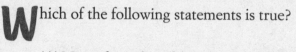

**W**hich of the following statements is true?

(A) Moses from the Bible was a major figure in US history.

(B) Slavery wasn't horrible if your master was nice.

(C) A Texas school district last year voted to ban the book *The Hate U Give*, and another Texas school district recently banned a book that included two boys kissing.

If you guessed C, you're (sadly) right! And you're light-years ahead of the adults who serve on the Texas State Board of Education, who have concluded that Moses influenced the US Constitution (he didn't) and that slavery can be described as anything other than a crime against humanity (wrong again).

The Texas State Board of Education is responsible for

approving textbooks and setting curriculum standards for more than five million public school kids across Texas. Yes, what you learn in school, the kinds of books you are assigned, the number of paintbrushes in the art room or test tubes in the science lab are all in some way determined by elected officials. And for decades, the Texas State Board of Education injected straight lies into the classroom.

Back in 1995, I attended a public meeting of this rather bland-sounding body, and I was riveted.

The same extreme right-wing Republican agenda that had swept George W. Bush into the governor's mansion also changed the balance of power on the fifteen-member State Board of Education. The newly elected members objected to the poems of the great African American Harlem Renaissance writer Langston Hughes, and to anything that smacked of equal rights for women, environmentalism, or negative portrayals of slavery, to name just a few.

Though it was 1995, I felt like I had traveled back in time to the 1950s.

I was outraged by what I was hearing. I scanned the room, looking for allies other than my friend Harriet Peppel, who had urged me to come see this circus for myself. Most of those in attendance were with the textbook industry, and they were simply trying to figure out what kind of books they could sell in Texas.

Where was this lunacy coming from? I had started reading more about the Christian Coalition, and it was like running down a rabbit hole. The more I discovered, the clearer it became that what was happening at the State

Board of Education was part of something broader. One of the founders of the Christian Coalition, the TV preacher Pat Robertson, used anxieties about a changing America to enlist support; he'd reach into of a grab bag of fears and toss out anything and everything he thought would stick. His warning that feminism "encourages women to leave their husbands, kill their children, practice witchcraft, destroy capitalism, and become lesbians" summed up the philosophy of the Christian Coalition. Another popular televangelist, Jerry Falwell, was crystal clear about their intentions, preaching, "I hope I live to see the day when, as in the early days of our country, we won't have any public schools. The churches will have taken them over again and Christians will be running them." It all reminded me of that day in sixth grade when Mrs. Powers called me out for not praying with the rest of the class, times a trillion. This was unconstitutional, backward, and wrong. The worst part was that they were well on their way to achieving these goals.

I was on fire. I wanted to turn to people and say, "Does everybody know what's going on? Isn't somebody going to do something about this?"

Then I realized: What if that somebody was me?

I'd never started anything other than the odd food co-op and antipollution group, but I realized that if I didn't do it, it probably wasn't going to happen. I mulled it over. On the one hand, our family had no savings and no house and we had three young kids in school and I was clueless about where to start. On the other hand, when I talked to Kirk about it, he cheerfully supported me. I've had a lot of harebrained schemes in my life, and he's gone along with every one of them. I was just so mad, and very ready to raise hell. I decided to go for it.

The first thing I did was make up a name, the Texas Freedom Alliance, and I typed up a mission statement. My goal was to organize Texans in support of public education. I found a group in Washington, the Alliance for Justice, that helped folks start nonprofits.

A few of us started the group in my living room, then found someone to temporarily donate a tiny office. My grandmother Nona wrote our first check, for a hundred dollars. It has to be the only check she ever wrote in her life for that much money. My kids were some of our earliest volunteers, helping put together flyers and mailing them out to people we knew. My sister held the first house party, and we were off.

I had just the beginnings of a plan, but every time I had to explain it to someone, it got a little bit clearer—we wanted to keep religion out of the public schools and make sure our kids

> **Every successful movement relies on a team of people. Who do you want on your team?**

were getting an education that was based on historical and scientific truths. Just like with Mom's campaign, we spoke with anyone and everyone who would welcome us. A lot of Texans were frustrated with the rightward political drift and looking for a place to pitch in.

Our unofficial motto was "Wherever two or more are gathered together!" Harriet and I drove all over Texas and, fortunately, joined forces with Janis Pinelli, another former Ann Richards volunteer. Not only did Janis have a car big enough for all three of us to ride around (and change clothes) in; she was also a licensed accountant and helped me figure out how to set up the books and create a board of directors, which all legitimate nonprofit organizations must have.

The farther we traveled, the more horror stories we heard. But there was even trouble close to home.

Round Rock, Texas, a suburb of Austin, is known for having an excellent school system. People would move there and commute to Austin just so their kids could go to the Round Rock public schools. Suddenly, after the 1994 elections, residents faced radical and unwelcome changes to the schools: the superintendent was fired, school board members were tossed out, and reading lists were rewritten. That was the breaking point for parents who weren't typical political activists. They got angry and were determined to fight back against what was happening.

Coincidentally, Round Rock had a well-known, well-respected young adult author right there in the district: Louis Sachar. He wrote books you may have read in school like *The Boy Who Lost His Face*, *Holes*, and our family's favorite, the hilarious Wayside School series. But here in his hometown, the local school board was trying to prevent young people from reading his work. When I spoke with him, I was shocked that anyone would think this mild-mannered author, whose books encouraged young people to read, could be a negative influence on kids. We were so lucky to have him in Texas.

The craziness of what was happening was so profound that we decided to make a documentary. This was long before smartphones with video cameras and editing tools. A couple of our friends made it for next to nothing, and it gave us an excuse to speak to groups. We'd show this ten-minute film, then give our spiel and try to recruit members.

We also battled at textbook hearings, bringing scientists to testify on the importance of accurate science books, and blasting out the most outrageous statements by school board members to the press. At one point some board members wanted to remove a photograph from a textbook of a nicely dressed woman walking out the door of her house, carrying a briefcase and waving to her family, saying it encouraged women to leave their children. We tipped off the *Today* show, and it made for great television.

Folks were definitely starting to take notice, including a right-wing group that had a similar name. They threatened to sue us if we didn't "cease and desist" calling ourselves the Texas Freedom Alliance. At least our scrappy group in Texas was on folks' radar! Even better, being pressured by them gave us a great chance to start a statewide renaming contest and get reporters to write stories about us in the press. That is how we became the Texas Freedom Network (TFN) and picked up some new supporters in the process.

**Can you think of a time you turned a problem into an opportunity?**

It was exciting and fulfilling to build something from nothing—especially something that might actually make a difference. Everywhere we went, we met people who were eager to help. By bringing together teachers, parent activists, and students across the state, our motley crew began to stand up for public schools. We also started organizing an unexpected group: religious leaders. We started the Texas Faith Network with Baptist preachers who had been fighting the takeover of the Southern Baptist Convention by the Far Right. They felt strongly that their religion should be disconnected from politics and government (a radical idea from . . . the US Constitution!).

When religious leaders spoke about moral issues, people listened, and their references to the Bible would shut down the opposition in ways I certainly couldn't. They became critical to our organizing efforts, voicing their support for LGBTQ rights and public education. Father Bill Davis, a Catholic priest from Houston, would ask me before public events, "Are we supposed to wear our sin-fighting suits?" Bill always came in his clerical collar unless otherwise notified.

Along the way I made my fair share of mistakes and learned just how hard it can be to get an organization off the ground and raise funds. I soon learned the truth of the saying, "If you want money, ask someone for advice. If you want advice, ask someone for money." There were plenty of folks (especially men) who didn't want to write a check but were happy to tell me how we should have organized. We had even made a last-ditch effort to raise money from a wealthy woman in Dallas—eight hours in Janis's car round trip—but came up short.

By the fall, we were out of cash. TFN was barely six

Austin, 1995, with the first volunteers for the Texas Freedom Network.

months old and on its last legs. Then, on Halloween, the phone rang at the office. I was wearing my Maleficent head-dress with entwined horns and a sweeping black cape, my eyes painted with black and purple makeup.

"I'm calling for Cecile, from the Leland Fikes Foun-dation in Dallas," said a woman's voice on the other end. Suddenly I remembered that one of the many requests for money we'd sent had been to the Fikes Foundation.

"We received your grant proposal, and I just have one question: What font did you use?"

Was this a trick question? Crazily enough, I knew. It was Footlight MT Bold. I've always had a thing for how printed materials look, and this was before the days when the Internet gave you a million options. It was important to me that anything we sent out looked good, and the font I'd picked was clean and classy. That's the beauty of running your own organization: you get to weigh in on everything from the logo to how to arrange the chairs at a meeting. I'd learned from Mom that there were a million ways to do something, but only one right way. So I told the caller.

"Great!" she said. "I love that font. I want to use it. Oh, and by the way, the foundation approved your grant. We'll send you the paperwork and have a check to you in a couple of weeks."

"Yessss!" I screamed at the office. This was our first legitimate grant. It meant we could make payroll through the end of the year, and maybe even be on the road to survival. That phone call gave me the confidence that we could keep going.

There was no guarantee when I'd started the Texas Freedom Network in my living room months earlier that it would ever make it. But if I hadn't given it a shot, I would have spent the rest of my life wondering what might have been. I stayed for three years and built it into a small but mighty organization.

Eventually, though, I started to feel that it was time to move on. Kirk and I were ready to leave town for the next challenge. I found a brilliant organizer to take over the reins of TFN, so when Kirk got a job in Washington, DC, it seemed like a good place to make a new start.

If there's one common theme that runs throughout my life, it's strong, resilient women. My grandmothers, each in their own very different ways, were tough and pioneering. My mother broke the mold. And at every job I've ever had, I've tried to work for someone who could teach me something—and more often than not, that someone has been a woman. For all these inspiring women, it wasn't as if the world just threw open the door and invited them in. Each one has been a disrupter in one way or another. They've made trouble, broken the rules, and challenged authority—and no one more than Nancy Pelosi, two-time Speaker of the US House of Representatives. The Speaker of the House is so powerful that it is second in the presidential line of succession, after the vice president.

> **Who are the inspiring women in your life?**

We had been living in Washington, DC, for a while now, but I had never worked in Congress. The people I did know on Capitol Hill had all been there for years and knew the ropes, so I was surprised when I was approached in 2001 about working in Nancy Pelosi's office. That whole world was a mystery to me. But President George W. Bush was in the White House by then, and it seemed like we were settling in for a rough few years. I wanted to be somewhere I could have a greater impact, so I decided to give it a try.

During my job interview, I was thinking, *This is crazy—why would they hire me when so many experienced people would kill for this job?* But they seemed to think my knowledge of the progressive organizing world would come in handy, and they brought me on, along with the brainiest bunch of people I've ever worked with.

Our office was so cramped you couldn't so much as sharpen your pencil without everyone else noticing. I was constantly aware of my shortcomings, though none of my colleagues ever made me feel inadequate. I was in awe of the people I worked with; they seemed to know everything about government. But mostly, I was blown away by Nancy Pelosi.

No one gets to be the highest-ranking woman in the history of our country without being enormously driven and willing to upset every convention, including the notion that men are forever destined to be in charge. She read every briefing memo, every policy paper, every headline—and expected her staff to do the same. Somehow she managed not only to beat us all to work in the morning but also to keep on top of all five of her kids, their spouses, and every grandkid. She would implore us at the end of the day, "Go home and see your family! Get out!" even though she never did.

She took sometimes unpopular positions and was tough enough to back her words with action, like her opposition to the disastrous war in Iraq. By the time of the vote on October 11, 2002, she had convinced a majority of Democrats in the House of Representatives to vote against the war. That was no small feat, considering that the majority of Democrats in the Senate voted for it. That was the Nancy Pelosi I have experienced time and time again, who knows her mind and does not back down.

Even though at times I felt like I was in over my head, I also felt at home working for Nancy. She reminded me so much of Mom. Both had raised kids and done what society expected of them before they had the chance to become political leaders. Both were impatient to make sure that the next generation of women did not have to wait so long.

My mother said often, "Life isn't fair, but government should be." There are countless stories of women who run for office because they believe exactly that—like Congresswoman Jan Schakowsky of Illinois, who got her start as a young housewife leading a campaign to put expiration dates on food in the grocery store, and Congresswoman Stephanie Murphy of Florida, who was inspired to challenge an incumbent endorsed by the National Rifle Association after a 2016 gun massacre at a Florida nightclub. Women aren't usually in it for the glory; they're in it to get something done.

And it's a good thing they are, because Congress on the whole is a macho, "guys hanging out with guys" kind of place. When Barbara Boxer was elected to the US Senate, there wasn't even a women's bathroom near the Senate floor—and that was in 1993! For many women in Congress, once they leave work for the day, they're back at their house, doing homework with their kids or catching up on the legislation they want to pass. But the men, even with their partisan differences, drink together, work out together; in Texas they hunt and fish together. There is no harder social circle to break into.

Like a lot of women in office, Nancy didn't get where she is because someone picked her; she got there because she decided to run and then was determined to succeed.

When I started working for her, the Democrats were the minority party—there were more Republicans in the House of Representatives, so they had the majority, and the Republican leader was Speaker of the House. Still, the party in the minority also elects a leader. When Nancy decided to run for Democratic leader, the odds were against her, but she devised a thorough plan to win over the support of her caucus. And she won.

Nancy has a deep grasp of history and enormous respect for the institutions of government and Congress. The day she was elected Democratic leader, she also became part of the congressional leadership made up of the two highest-ranking members of each party in the House and Senate. As is customary, the president invited the group to the White House. When Nancy came to work the next day, she was still processing what her election meant. Back in her offices on the second floor of the Capitol, she described the emotion of going to the meeting with the president. I've never forgotten what she told us that day. "I was so aware, walking through the gates and into the White House, of the hard work and sacrifice of prior generations of women. The suffragists," she said, recalling the activists who, more than 140 years after America's founding, had secured women's right to vote. "And all the women who broke barriers. As I sat at the table with the president and the top leaders of Congress, I realized that it was the very first time a woman had ever been at this table. It was as if women from throughout history, women who had made this possible, were there with me. And all around me, I felt their presence." She often quoted Congresswoman Lindy Boggs from Louisiana, a mentor of hers, who implored women, "Know thy power!"

To the surprise of no one, Nancy's workday did not end at five p.m. She spent every additional waking hour helping her colleagues stay in Congress—flying out to support them in their districts, organizing private lunches for them, and advising them in the way only she could. If you could show her your campaign wasn't about just you, she would move heaven and earth to help. No matter your gender, race, or ethnicity, she believed what mattered was your commitment and connection to your community. The way she saw it, if you were going to come to Congress, you'd better be ready to work for the folks back home. Besides which, she knew that this was the only way Congress would ever look like the people of America. That's especially true today, with a rising generation of new members of Congress, including young people, women, and people of color, that is more diverse than any that has come before.

I had been on Capitol Hill for less than two years when the organizing bug bit once again. This time I wanted to use the experience I'd gained to help progressive organizations work together and unite their voter outreach efforts so they could more effectively elect leaders to office. That's how I found myself starting what became America Votes, the largest collection of progressive grassroots organizations working together to register, educate, and turn out voters.

But I didn't limit my organizing to work or to grownups. Around this time, my twins were in elementary school. Hannah was in the Girl Scouts and Daniel was in the Cub Scouts. Hannah spent the Girl Scout year doing three things: getting ready for the cookie sale, selling the cookies, and tabulating the sales. I'm sure this is not the experience of every Girl Scout troop, but meanwhile Daniel was in the Cub Scouts, and he didn't have to sell a thing. Daniel and I carved a car for the Pinewood Derby and competed with Cub Scouts from all around the area. His den was taking bike rides along the C&O Canal, learning about rocket ships from astronauts, and volunteering at Loaves and Fishes, the local soup kitchen.

Finally, one day I'd had it. I said to Hannah, "What if we started our own organization, one where we didn't have to sell cookies and could do the cool kinds of things the Cub Scouts do?"

Hannah was game, so along with a half dozen of her friends from her fourth-grade class, we got ourselves organized. The girls met and determined they needed a name and a T-shirt. They decided to call themselves the Future Women Presidents, and one of the artistic moms in the group designed the shirts. We went camping and learned how to make a fire and cook outdoors. They painted a mural at a community center. They hiked, recycled, visited the National Museum of Women in the Arts, and then, through a miraculous series of events, got an insider's tour of the White House. It seemed only fitting for the Future Women Presidents!

As the girls moved out of elementary school and into junior high, the FWP dissolved. It's nice to think that early on they had the chance to think big thoughts, learn some self-sufficiency, and be proud of the women they would become.

In starting America Votes and Future Women Presidents, I learned one of the most important lessons of my life: don't wait for all the boats to get in the flotilla—just start moving. You may lose a few people, and others may join up along the way, but if you wait until everyone is 100 percent on board, you'll never get going. At a certain point you have to quit talking about it and start doing it.

I meet people all the time who are considering starting their own organizations, whether a student group on a college campus or a national initiative. If you're thinking of giving it a shot, here are a few of the things I learned.

First, be practical: Set a goal so you can achieve something concrete. In the beginning it's going to be the small wins. I knew I could not start the Texas Freedom Network by myself, so my initial goal was to raise enough money in the first three months to pay an assistant and myself.

Second, you have to be willing to ask for money. And believe me, it's a great skill to have. It tests your proof of concept: if you can find people willing to pitch in a few dollars, then you are onto something. And there aren't any shortcuts worth taking. How many nonprofit meetings have

I been in where someone says, "Maybe we could get Oprah or Lin-Manuel Miranda or Beyoncé to do a fund-raiser for us." That's just not how it works. Raising money isn't only about getting an influx of cash; it's about being able to prove that other people support the idea you're working on. It's about building a following.

Third, for better or worse, when you start and run your own organization, you own all the successes and all the failures. Big risk, big gain. It's like being an entrepreneur, only you're not trying to make a profit.

Fourth, master the organizing rules of the road: Always have a room that's half the size you need, with half the chairs you need, so you can guarantee meetings will be standing room only. When you are starting out with new leaders, make sure everyone has the chance to speak. That will be the single best test of whether the meeting went well: Did they get a chance to give their point of view? Besides, you learn more from listening than from speaking. Of course, getting people in a room is 20 percent of the work; the other 80 percent is having something meaningful for them to do after they walk out the door. And no matter what you do, never forget the basics: Provide name tags; start on time and end on time; have a next step for the group; have fun. Remember, "If I can't dance, I don't want to be part of your revolution."

There are a ton of great ideas floating around the universe, but the ones that end up becoming reality are those someone commits to doing, no matter what. Why not you?

# 6

## Say Yes

**W**e had just finally bought a house in Washington, DC, the kids were settled in school, and I was immersed in my job at America Votes when I got a call in fall 2005 to see if I'd be interested in taking over as president of Planned Parenthood. My first thought was *Are you kidding?* I had an inkling of what an enormous undertaking this would be.

I called Kirk. He's always been the most supportive, positive person in my life. Sometimes I think that if I called and said we needed to pack up and go to Mars, he would just ask, "What do I need to bring?"

"That sounds great! I love New York!" was his response. He knew the job was huge and complicated, but he pushed me to go for it.

A couple of weeks later I was standing in front of my closet, trying to pick out the right outfit to wear for the biggest interview of my professional career. At every other job I'd had, I was creating something new, but Planned

Parenthood was a huge organization—one in five women in America has been to Planned Parenthood for health care—and it had a hundred-year legacy.

The interview was at an office building a few minutes away from America Votes, where I would meet with the national search committee—which in and of itself sounded overwhelming. I went to a nearby coffee shop to gather my thoughts, but instead I freaked out.

I started running through my list of "why nots": *This is the wrong time. My kids are still in school. We could never move.* Here I was, barely in the first round of interviews, already worrying about what would happen if I got the job. I was on the verge of calling the search firm and telling them I'd take a pass.

Instead I did what any grown woman would do: I called my mom.

I told her what I was about to do, then immediately launched into all the reasons I wasn't the person for the job: I'd never run anything this big before, let alone an established organization that millions of people counted on for health care each year. Why on earth would they even consider me for the position?

Mom was just not having it. I'm sure she was thinking about all the women she'd known who'd sabotaged themselves because of fear and self-doubt, and she wasn't about to let me off easily. "Cecile, you will never know unless you try. And let's face it: you only get one life, and this is it. Besides, Planned Parenthood is doing more for women's health than any organization in America! How exciting!"

Her voice still rings in my head, asking, "What's the worst thing that could happen?" She was right. I could try for it and not get the job; I could handle

that. Or I could get the job and be a colossal failure, which would be pretty bad, but even then I'd eventually get over it and do something else.

Though I was sure I'd never get the job, I showed up for the interview and found ten people sitting around the conference table, ready to ask questions. I didn't know any of them personally, but Mom's advice had calmed me down. And besides, knowing deep down that this was a long shot actually helped—I felt like I had nothing to lose.

I loved the search committee right away. One of the members was a legend in the world of reproductive rights, Jill June. She ran Planned Parenthood in Iowa, and though she looked like a kindly grandmother, she was as fearless as they came. "We're the very best at what we do, providing reproductive health care for women," she explained. "But we keep losing ground in the political arena, and we can't count on another organization to fix it for us. We need to get back to our movement roots. Are you interested?"

You may be wondering what women's health has to do with "the political arena" or why it should matter how the White House and members of Congress feel about Planned Parenthood. For one thing, Planned Parenthood depends on government funding to provide health care to millions of women, men, and young people across the country.

That's the sound bite, but what does it really mean in the lives of women and their families? To start, women have different health needs than men. One important aspect of women's medical care is to get screened regularly for breast cancer. Also, women's reproductive organs, where babies develop and grow, require checkups every year from specialized health care providers so they can stay healthy. But there's a lot more.

When men and women have sex, women can get pregnant. But if they don't want to have a baby, they need to use birth control. There are lots of forms of birth control— condoms that men or women can wear or pills women can swallow or devices that health care providers can implant inside women's bodies. Planned Parenthood teaches people about and provides them with all their birth control options, to keep everyone healthy and help people prevent unintended pregnancies. Sometimes a woman gets pregnant but decides she cannot carry out the pregnancy—maybe the baby developing inside her body, called a fetus, would endanger her life, or maybe she didn't mean to get pregnant. When that happens, women have the right to choose to have an abortion to end the pregnancy.

Planned Parenthood centers offer the full range of reproductive health care services—gynecological exams, family planning, birth control, cancer screening, and abortion—to 2.4 million people along with sex education to young people and communities so they can learn about things like safer sex, birth control, and healthy relationships. And half of all Planned Parenthood centers are in parts of the country where it's nearly impossible and too expensive to find a doctor who can provide these services.

So what do the White House and Congress have to do with all this? Much more than they should. First, there is a government program called Medicaid. It helps pay for doctors' visits and medication for people with low incomes. Since Planned Parenthood serves a lot of women who don't make enough money to pay for doctors' visits, some of its funding ends up coming from the government, through Medicaid. When lawmakers in power threaten to cut off funds for Planned Parenthood, what they are really doing is hurting lots of patients who have nowhere else to turn for medical care.

And then there's the issue of women's rights. For most of American history, women haven't had reproductive freedom, which means the right to choose when to have a baby or whether to have a baby, or to decide to end a pregnancy. But that changed in the last century as women organized and demanded those and other rights. In 1973 the United States Supreme Court ruled on the case *Roe v. Wade*, which made abortion legal nationwide. This means that all of us have the right to control our own bodies and the right to make the best health care decisions for ourselves.

You'd think that would have settled the matter, but it hasn't. Opponents of the right of pregnant people to make their own health decisions have tried to undermine the law in every way they could over the last forty-five years. In addition to health care services for women, a big part of what Planned Parenthood does is support the laws that protect rights to birth control, safe family planning services, reproductive care, and abortion.

It was clear to me that the job would have a steep learning curve and demand more than full-time attention. On the other hand, I could be a good partner in a lot of the things they wanted to do. I was more than interested.

We had a great conversation, and when Patricio Gonzales, a Planned Parenthood leader serving women on the Rio Grande border in Texas, spoke of the struggles to provide services in an area of the country I knew so well, he touched my heart. So many women in the Rio Grande Valley depended on Planned Parenthood for health care, and if they lost it—which was definitely a possibility—Patricio was afraid they would have no option but to go over the border to Mexico. (Those fears would become a reality years later, when politicians in Texas forced health centers across the state to close, giving some women no choice but to leave the state for birth control and abortions.)

I left the interview thinking, *This could be really exciting.* So you might think I was thrilled to get the call saying they wanted me back for a second interview. Oh, no: I went through all the same anxieties, only this time they were worse. Now it seemed like I really might get the job—and then what? I was terrified.

Somehow I gutted up and showed up again. They were definitely interested. The search firm called me almost immediately after I left that interview and made me an offer. When I hesitated, the woman on the other end of the phone jumped right in. "How are you *not* going to do this?" she asked.

She was right. I took the leap and said yes, having only the slightest idea what I was stepping into.

I knew Kirk was ready to go to New York; we'd had plenty of Washington. Lily was getting ready to graduate and head off to college. But I still had to break it to Hannah and Daniel. Hannah and I were driving in the car when I decided to tell her. Why is it always in the car where the most difficult conversations happen between parents and kids?

"Hannah, I know how happy you are here in Washington, but I decided to take the job with Planned Parenthood." Gulp. Silence.

"You and Daniel can finish out ninth grade, but I'll go on up to New York and find us a place to live. It will be great, though I know it's a big change."

In her younger years Hannah was the master of the silent treatment, and this was no exception. In contrast to her tears at age six when we left Texas, this time she sat there like a stone. I have a terrible habit of filling any silence, so I kept talking. "Just think—you can meet all kinds of new people and go to a new school. And your friends will definitely come and visit!"

Eventually she came around, but it wasn't easy. It would be years before we could look back on this move, like all our others, and agree it was the right thing for us as a family.

Besides being worried about the kids, I was concerned about leaving my job and my staff at America Votes. After all, I'd started the organization, and it felt like a betrayal to leave it and those good people behind. And then there was a new kind of worry I'd never before had to consider.

Part of the routine for a new Planned Parenthood leader is to have a security team evaluate their physical safety, I'm sorry to say. Abortion opponents have threatened and even killed doctors and activists who support a woman's right to end her pregnancy. I'd never had a job where security was part of the daily routine but quickly realized this was standard practice for Planned Parenthood CEOs around the country. It didn't give me pause, but I realized that life with Planned Parenthood required a different level of awareness—for me, the kids, and Kirk. And I would come to learn that making sure your house is secure isn't a lot of help once you start getting recognized in public. More than once I've been confronted on the street or at an airport, like the time a man—and they are almost always men—walked up as I was sitting at the gate, told me he was praying for me, and handed me a completely nutty self-published religious book. He stood there for what felt like forever, and all I could think was *How can I possibly get myself out of here?*

The kids and Kirk were back in Washington when I started my new job in early 2006. The minute I said yes to the job, I knew my life was about to change in a million ways. This was one: when you work for Planned Parenthood, you spend more time talking about sex than you could possibly imagine. It comes up in meetings and emails—like my first all-staff meeting. Right off the bat, one of the staffers stood up and cut right to the chase: "I was wondering, what's your plan to make sexual pleasure a universal value in the United States?"

I'm sure my expression was like the squirrel in the movie

*Ice Age*: huge eyes and utter shock. "Okay, well, you've got me there. I'm going to have a lot to learn from you!"

As soon as I took the job, my kids became the go-to sources of information about Planned Parenthood for their peers. Lily, who had left for college in Massachusetts, suddenly found that high school friends everywhere were reaching out to her, looking for a place to get birth control or a way to be in touch with Planned Parenthood. She called me in October that first year. "Mom, my friend Sarah just called me because her friend needs to get birth control. Do you know where the closest place is in Indianapolis?" I went to look up our clinic information and it dawned on me: there had to be a better way for us to be there for young people. I couldn't call back every college student in the United States, nor did most of them know to call Lily.

At the time, Planned Parenthood had a national website, but it was exclusively focused on political activism, not on providing health care. If you were trying to find birth control in, say, Oklahoma City, it would have been a challenge. Being able to get first-rate health care information or find a health center 24/7 was at the core of our mission. I knew if we got it right, the Internet and Planned Parenthood could be a match made in heaven. I just wasn't sure where to start, so I put together a team to look into it.

As we suspected, about 95 percent of the visitors to our website were looking for something we were not providing: a way to find the closest Planned Parenthood health center.

Convincing folks in our 128 affiliates—all with their own distinct cultures—that the need to connect with millions more people online was an opportunity, not a threat, took some doing. Planned Parenthood had been started by troublemaking, fiercely independent leaders all across the country, and the last thing they wanted was the national offices in New York and Washington telling them what to do. Plus, people who are born to challenge authority do it every chance they get—including in their own organization. But we did it, building the only national reproductive rights website that receives more than 72 million visits a year, lets patients make appointments on their mobile phones day or night, and provides health information twenty-four hours a day, seven days a week, in English and Spanish.

Meanwhile, Planned Parenthood's most important work was happening at health centers across America. I was itching to get out of our office and get to know the organization from a different perspective.

There was so much to learn and see for myself—most important, the kind of heroic work by staff and volunteers in the states. As Jill June had mentioned back in my first job interview, Planned Parenthood leaders were not only providing health care but were also battling daily to protect access to all the services Planned Parenthood provides.

One important battle was the fight for safe, legal abortion in South Dakota, one of the most politically conservative states in the country. The local Planned Parenthood CEO, Sarah Stoesz, had an essential combination of skills: she knew a lot about political organizing from her early days working for a US senator, and she had experience delivering first-class health care in some of the most remote areas of the country, where opposition to our work by elected officials was high.

Just as I arrived, the South Dakota legislature passed a bill making all abortion illegal. It would have been a disaster for women and families across the state, and especially for South Dakota's most marginalized people, like those with low incomes and the indigenous community. It looked hopeless. But the bill was also unconstitutional, because the Supreme Court had ruled decades earlier that abortion is legal. This meant that Planned Parenthood could sue, and bring the new law to court for a judge to overturn. Sarah disagreed with that strategy.

"We have got to fight this on the ground," she told me. "What they're trying to do is clearly unconstitutional, but rather than go to court, we have the right to take this unconscionable law straight to the voters in South Dakota and convince them to overturn it. That's what we need to do."

That tactic sounded crazy to me. After all, if the law was unconstitutional, why not sue? "This is an opportunity to fundamentally challenge the belief that people in South Dakota—people anywhere, for that matter—want abortion to be illegal," Sarah said. "I know it'll be hard to win, but we have to try. A lawsuit should be our last resort."

Sarah was persuasive and, as it turned out, completely right. It was a shrewd decision, but also an optimistic vision. She knew her people, the people of South Dakota, cared about women's rights. And she also knew that a law this important, and controversial, had to have the backing of the voters, making the choice—yes or no—on the ballot with their eyes wide open. If the decision was left up to judges sitting in a remote courtroom, people wouldn't feel as connected to it.

She collected the signatures to get the law on the ballot and raised the money for a statewide effort to repeal the law. She hired and trained organizers to go door to door in South Dakota, explaining to voters that this legislation would take the right away from women and their families to make important decisions about pregnancy. Sarah took me to visit the health center in Sioux Falls, where courageous staff continued to provide care for women. We also met some of the organizers on the campaign; these young women were fearless. After talking to complete strangers about abortion in South Dakota, they could do anything.

Sarah was the first to show me that people are capable of holding two important ideas at the same time. "A person may have their own deeply felt opinion about abortion," she explained. "They may not believe it is a choice they would make. But they are also able to respect the decisions that each woman, or family, may make themselves." A mother who ended up making a television ad for the campaign reflected just that. She and her husband had been overjoyed to learn that she was pregnant with twins. But after discovering a serious medical complication, they made the tough decision to terminate one of the pregnancies so the other twin could survive. She had never been an activist before, but she decided that if telling her story could help someone else, it was worth it.

When the voters in South Dakota went to the polls, they

voted down the legislation overwhelmingly. What Sarah believed was proven true not only on that Election Day but subsequently on a second effort in South Dakota, another in Mississippi, two ballot measures in North Dakota, and in Colorado. It was an important political lesson—if you provide the best, most far-reaching services that people rely on, they will support your work when it's threatened by political leaders who try to shut it down. And beyond the doors of Planned Parenthood clinics, it showed that people's ability to respect a woman's right to make her own decisions about a pregnancy, including abortion, just might surprise you.

> People who don't believe in abortion don't have to have one, but they shouldn't stop any woman from exercising her right to one. What can you do to protect the right of all people to make their own health decisions?

One of the best-kept secrets about Planned Parenthood is that it is the largest provider of sex education in the United States. For so many young people, it is their only source of honest, nonjudgmental information about their bodies and their lives. Planned Parenthood educators are out on the front lines in schools and communities, where often no one else is. Sex education is really important, not only for the obvious reasons that it's helpful to know about sex, bodies, and relationships. Sex education teaches young folks about how to have healthy, consensual sex and relationships, including how to avoid unintended pregnancies and prevent the spread of sexually transmitted infections (STIs). Planned Parenthood offers testing and treatment for STIs and support to anyone who walks in its door—no matter how much money you make, where you live, where you come from, who you love, or how you identify.

One of the first educators I met was Irwin Royster, a young man who was running Planned Parenthood's Ophelia Egypt Health Clinic. His enthusiasm was irresistible. There, in the shadow of the nation's capital, with the highest rate of HIV infection in the country, he ran an after-school program connected with the Planned Parenthood clinic. He had convinced a small strip mall to give him an abandoned sporting goods storefront, which he filled with secondhand furniture and cast-off computers. (I would later donate our foosball table to the cause.)

Working twenty-hour days, with barely two nickels to rub together, Irwin and his team helped high-risk teens in the area get testing, counseling, and health care. Most of all, he was providing young people in Anacostia with a safe place to go after school. Some of these teens became educators themselves and were a lifeline for their fellow students. I started getting excited about the opportunity to connect these young people to others across the country.

In Kalamazoo, Michigan, it all came together. I was sitting with a group of local teens who were part of a Planned Parenthood–sponsored teen sex education program. They told me about learning everything there was to know about birth control, consent, sexually transmitted infections and how to prevent them, and more. They had testified before school board meetings and had publicly spoken out in favor of comprehensive sex education. In small, conservative-leaning Kalamazoo, that wasn't easy. I was captivated.

Lindsay Swisher, a high school senior about to graduate, told me, "When I started as a teen peer educator four years ago, I was really shy." But after being part of Planned Parenthood, she said, "I can talk to anyone about anything. It has changed my life."

These teens weren't simply sex educators; they were leaders, and they belonged at the center of everything we did. Every investment we could make in them would help build our organization, and more than that, our movement. We decided to invite a group of teens from across the country to speak at our national meeting, where hundreds of the most important Planned Parenthood leaders came together.

That first time, I wasn't really sure how it was going to go. The great thing about bringing teens into the meeting was that they were going to shake things up—for better or worse! What happened that first year, and ever since, turned out to be magical. Leaders who had been asking me, "Why don't young people get involved and appreciate all we've done?" were now seeing them in action. And it was obvious how much the established crowd had to learn from the next generation of Planned Parenthood activists, who were without a doubt the most diverse group in our organization. Today I hardly ever hear those questions from longtime Planned Parenthood leaders. Where are the young people? They're everywhere!

But despite the world-class health care, the great organizing, and the young leaders at Planned Parenthood, there was no escaping the fact that our biggest threat was political. Elected officials who were Republican, by and large, wanted to shut us down. We were having a hard time even with our advocates on Capitol Hill. We had to show elected officials that there were millions of Planned Parenthood supporters who would come out and vote for them if they championed women's reproductive health care. We had to back up our principles with action. We needed to build our grassroots support so that members of Congress heard from people back in their home districts.

We also started to get involved in presidential campaigns. In 2008 Senator John McCain, the Republican nominee, wanted to outlaw abortion, so the general election would be a real contest of ideals. The Democratic nominee, Barack Obama, supported reproductive health care. His campaign was an unprecedented chance to mobilize our millions of supporters, and we made the most of it, training organizers and recruiting as many new volunteers as we could. From college campuses to rock concerts, anywhere two or more were gathered together, we signed them up. On election night, when Barack Obama won, I cried and celebrated with the rest of America—and I breathed an extra sigh of relief that our big bet had paid off.

Four years later Planned Parenthood had grown, as had our ability to impact policy and politics. This time President Obama was facing a tough opponent in Governor Mitt Romney from Massachusetts. Romney was known as a moderate—he and his wife had even come to Planned Parenthood events in support of women's issues.

But in March 2012 he made a crucial error. He boasted on television, "Planned Parenthood? We're going to get rid of that." That piece of video footage became a television ad that we ran across the country. And as the race tightened, it was clear that women were going to be key voters. President Obama and Mitt Romney met at Hofstra University in New York State for their second, pivotal debate.

I was backstage, watching with a handful of others who had been asked to be available to answer reporters' questions afterward. I heard President Obama say, "There are millions of women all across the country who rely on Planned Parenthood." I could hardly believe it. He proceeded to mention Planned Parenthood, and the work we did, three more times—not that I was counting!

It was the first time Planned Parenthood had been mentioned in a presidential debate, and President Obama went on to win the election with the largest support from women of any presidential candidate to date. Best of all, we had cracked the code, making sure that when politicians and the public thought about us, they knew who we were and what we did.

This came home to me a couple of days after that debate, when a woman came into our health center on the Gulf Coast Freeway in Houston. She didn't have a doctor, but she had found a lump in her breast and needed to see someone. The clinician welcomed her and said, "We're so glad you're here. May I ask who referred you?" The woman answered, "Well, I heard President Obama say on TV that you do breast exams. And that's why I'm here."

In my time at Planned Parenthood I've visited health centers from Brownsville, Texas, to Milwaukee, Wisconsin, and in every one the waiting rooms were full of women and young people who needed health care. I remember sitting across the desk from a health center manager in Mobile, Alabama, who had been a teen mom herself and was now counseling women on their options. "Planned Parenthood is straight-up health care," she said. "The way it should be. This is a judgment-free zone." I've talked to nurses and doctors in Hawaii about the challenges of delivering health care to people away from the mainland, and in Alaska, where we once delivered birth control by float plane to a remote village in the Arctic Circle.

People ask me whether I am concerned for my safety when I'm on the road. The truth is, most of the people who stop me want to thank me or tell me why they love Planned Parenthood. There was the woman who chased me down on the airport tarmac in Texas to tell me she'd just been at the fund-raiser where I spoke and was inspired to call her parents and tell them she'd had an abortion years ago. And the soundboard operator at a big women's conference in Los Angeles—one of a small handful of men present—who stopped me backstage to tell me his wife and daughters go to Planned Parenthood, and he just had to get a picture. I

**Are there activists out there you want to thank? I bet they'd love to hear from you!**

learned never to shy away from telling people what you do. You crush myths, for others and for yourself.

Twelve years later I'm grateful every day that I went to that interview. Today the number of Planned Parenthood supporters has tripled, reaching more than 11 million. Nearly half are young people. Millions of appointments have been scheduled on mobile phones. The organization has invested in thousands of young people who are changing the world. And those young people have shepherded us into the twenty-first century. Most of all, I've been so fortunate to meet doctors, medical staff, clinic volunteers, and local leaders who, despite all the political attacks, continue to open the doors of Planned Parenthood health centers every single day, no matter what.

These days when someone asks me for career advice, some of the first words out of my mouth are the lessons I learned at Planned Parenthood: At every job, look for someone who can teach you something. Stay close to the people on the ground, and remember that you're never too big of a deal to knock on doors. Find something outside your job that brings you joy—don't look up years later and realize you missed out on the things you love. Know that there's no road map for social change—so keep making it up, don't get stuck or tied down, and never turn down a new opportunity. And never ever hold yourself back from accepting a big job or a big chance. You can and will figure it out—take it from me.

# 7

## What Would Ann Richards Do?

One of the best things about moving to New York City was that our apartment had room enough for Mom to visit as much as she wanted. Mom loved New York, and I couldn't wait for her to join us. But shortly after we moved in, she called with news that would change everything. Something in her throat had been bothering her for a while, and the doctors confirmed her fears: she had cancer of her esophagus, the tube that carries food from your mouth to your stomach.

Mom was scared but calm when she delivered the news. I was in a state of disbelief. This was not how I'd imagined the future. I had just started at Planned Parenthood and, selfishly, pictured us together in the city, with Mom fighting alongside me for women's rights. We had more adventures to take together. Plus, she was such a force in my children's lives. Things were always bigger, brighter, and funnier when she was around. How could she have cancer? It just didn't fit.

"We'll figure this out," she said.

We quickly discovered that hers was a really tough form of cancer, and she had to decide whether to fight or try to manage it for as long as she could.

My mother hated being sick. To her, it was a sign of personal failure, even if she knew logically how silly that was. In Texas the highest compliment, far greater than being told you're smart or well-educated, is being considered tough. In our football-obsessed culture straight out of *Friday Night Lights*, the greatest praise goes to someone who "plays hurt"—regardless of torn ligaments or broken fingers.

Mom subscribed to that school of thought. I cannot remember a time when any of us kids stayed home from school. It wasn't because she was a working mother and had to have us out of the house; it was because, no matter what, you were going to suck it up and go, even if you didn't feel good.

It was a lesson I also absorbed, to a fault. My own kids never missed a day of school unless the teacher called and said I had to come get one of them. Of course that philosophy has its drawbacks. One Christmas I was dragging Lily from place to place, rushing to finish shopping for gifts, when she said, "Mom, I really feel sick."

"We just have this one last stop at the music store. You'll be fine," I told her, only to have her throw up all over a gigantic bin of CDs. We haven't been back to Waterloo Records since.

Mom's view of sickness as a weakness surely came from her mother, who was strong as an ox and worked as hard as anyone I've ever known. Mom used to tell the story of the time she got a call at the governor's office from one of Nona's neighbors. "Ann, you are going to have to come get your mother. She's up on the roof again, cleaning out the gutters. I don't think that's safe for an eighty-year-old woman." Mom just laughed—there was no way her mother was coming down from that roof until she was good and ready.

My mother walked through fire many times, and as she liked to say, "The fire lost." There was no doubt in my mind that she would beat cancer too. After the diagnosis, she made the decision to move to Houston for experimental treatment at M. D. Anderson Cancer Center, and in between trips for my new job, I visited her there. We spent the time watching *Project Runway*, which she found endlessly entertaining, and she laughed uncontrollably as we sat through the old movie *Blazing Saddles* one night, even as the powerful chemotherapy drugs coursed through her and weakened her. She admitted during one of those visits that she had suspected she was sick before she went on a long-planned trip to India, but she'd decided not to tell anyone for fear the doctors wouldn't let her go. When she got home from what would end up being her last adventure, she told me about visiting Varanasi, where Hindus cremate their dead—burn them to ashes in a religious ritual—on the banks of the Ganges River. "It was so important, Cecile," she said. "I have never been anywhere so spiritual." Clearly the experience had touched her deeply. I realize now that she was thinking about the end of her own life. Getting cancer was the first time Mom seemed to accept that there was such a thing as human frailty, and she understood that taking care of herself had to be her full-time job. She approached it with campaign-like determination and became interested in chi, the life force particularly important in systems of medical treatment from China.

When Mom was governor, her friend and partner in everything she did, Jane Hickie, made her a notepad with "Ann Richards: The Problem Lady" emblazoned at the top. That was what Mom used to call herself, since she had an answer for every problem. There were a lot of opinions in the world, but only one correct one: Mom's. And, truth be told, she was almost always right. When word spread that she was sick, she received desperate phone calls from people asking for advice, perhaps because subconsciously they realized it could be their last chance to get some Ann Richards wisdom. But after spending much of her life shaking hands with strangers, calling them "honey," she had finally learned to save her energy for herself. When someone called upon her for her time, she'd say, "Cecile, I'm just not going to do everything everyone wants me to—it's wasting my chi!" That was as close to self-care as she ever got.

After months of treatment, Mom went home to Austin. In the exit interview, one of her doctors said, "Ann, you've been a perfect patient. We feel really good that through radiation we've gotten the cancer, and now you can start to recover." Radiotherapy shoots powerful beams of radiation into the body to kill cancer cells, and it had made it impossible for her to eat anything for weeks. To provide her body with nutrients, Mom was relying on a feeding tube, which we were taking home. "I need you to get healthy, so we can do the final surgery," he said. Mom and I just looked at each other—it was impossible to imagine her recovering enough to have surgery.

As we were leaving, I saw Dr. Fan, Mom's doctor, who had really made an impression on her. Dr. Fan was brilliant, yet Mom was always in her business, giving her advice about her life, her decisions, and everything she needed to do. *Welcome to the family!*

"Thank you, Doctor," I told her. "You have been so good to Mom."

"Well, she's helped me, too, given me a lot of advice. Just be sure to let her know I traded in the old car and got a new Prius, just like she told me to."

My mother died only a few weeks later, in September 2006, at her home, in her own bed, with all of us at her side. She had made her own decisions, right to the end. She knew her own mind and was counting on us kids to respect that, and of course we did.

She'd already picked out a plot in the Texas State Cemetery, under an oak tree. Her gravestone, designed by her friend Robert Smith, is a piece of white marble that looks a whole lot like her famous pouffy white hairdo. It's smooth and welcoming, and Mom always dreamed that people might visit it and leave stones or charms—which they do.

Mom left us way too early in that she had so much more to give to this world. She often reminded us, "I'm not the baking-cookies kind of grandma," and she was right. But her love and devotion came through loud and clear. She set many of us on our path and left us a lot of life lessons. Lily summed it up best in her speech at Mom's memorial service: "Every time Mammy saw one of us grandkids, she would say, 'How's school?' And then she would ask, 'Are you the smartest one in the class?'

"And if we hedged in our reply, she would ask, 'Well, why not?' This might seem a little too demanding, but it wasn't. Because Mammy had learned the most important lesson of all, and she was teaching it to all of us. That lesson was simple: This is your life. It is the only one you get, so no excuses and no do-overs. If you make a mistake or fail at something, you learn from it, you get over it, and you move on. Your job is to be the very best person you can be, and to never settle for anything less.

"This message was not just given to her children and her grandchildren, but also in countless speeches and one-on-one conversations with thousands of

**What pushes you to be your "best person" every day?**

people, many of them young women, across this country. She delivered this message as only she could—with wit, with intensity, but most importantly, by example. Mammy was the very best person she could be every single day."

To see Mom evolve and change, right up to her very last years, was a gift for me. Plenty of people get more conservative and settled in their ways as they get older. She got more radical. During cancer treatment she had a team of doctors, all of whom were from other countries. She would say, "Can you believe these right-wing politicians who want to end immigration? Who in the hell do they think is going to keep them alive when they get old?"

The more years she spent in the fight for LGBTQ rights, civil rights, and so many other issues, the more outspoken she became. That was especially true of women's rights. Mom saw history repeating itself and was downright furious at the idea that her granddaughters' generation would have to refight the same battles she'd helped wage.

Once she left elected office, she was very much in demand as a speaker on the campaign trail, and candidates were constantly calling her and asking her to campaign for them. After years of helping so many Democrats, she made it absolutely clear: unless you were 100 percent pro-choice—supportive of a woman's right to an abortion—she wouldn't lift a finger. But if you championed women, she would travel to the ends of the earth for you.

Near the end of her life, Mom knew she had only a certain amount of time left, and she was determined to spend it fighting as fiercely as she could to leave behind a better world for us all. Before she was going to make a speech, she loved to call and read me parts that she had worked on and was really proud of. She had recently fallen in love with the irreverent words of the Irish American labor activist Mother Jones, and the more outrageous the quote, the better. "Listen to this: 'I'm not a humanitarian, I'm a hell-raiser!'" she read. "Don't you love that? And how about, 'Whatever your fight, don't be ladylike!'" One of her mantras was "Ask for forgiveness, not permission." She firmly believed in the idea that if you aren't making the powers that be a little nervous, demanding a seat at the table where decisions are made, you aren't doing your job.

Not a day goes by when I don't miss Mom. Some days I miss her so much I can hardly stand it. It catches me off guard, like the time I came across a video clip from an old interview. "You may go somewhere else and you may make a lot of money," she said, "but you will never receive the kind of gratification that you receive from looking someone in the eye who says, 'Thank you for helping make my life better.'" She made all of our lives better—those of us who knew and loved her, and so many people she never met.

Before she died, Mom decided that one way she could make a lasting difference was to start a girls' school. She'd had friends who started girls' schools in New York and California, and she thought, *Why not Texas?* That's how, one year later, the Ann Richards School for Young Women Leaders came to be: a public school in Austin with one of the most diverse student bodies in the city. It has been a resounding success; there are now young women scattered all over the country who are graduates of the Ann Richards School. Many of them are the first person in their family to go to college.

Recently I was back in Austin, and I had the chance to visit there. Crammed into a public school in South Austin, busting at the seams, eight-hundred-plus young girls and women are doing their thing. We saw the MakerSpace where, using a 3-D printer, girls were designing a habitat for outer space. I helped carry the wooden frames in the shop class where others were building pigpens for the local zoo. The drama troupe was onstage, practicing the upcoming play. "It's not easy to find plays written by women, with parts for girls," the leader explained, "but we are doing it." As we walked through the halls, graduating seniors talked to me about where they were hoping to go to college, since this is an expectation of the school—and every girl does. One was determined to be an engineer, and others were mathematicians. Most poignant were the questions. "Can you give me advice?" asked one bright-eyed girl. "What would you do if you just love EVERYTHING?" Each time I go back to visit, I feel it's the place where Mom's spirit truly lives.

Everywhere I go, I run into people who want to talk about Mom. Many recount how something she did or said changed their lives, how because of her, they decided to travel, run for office, or get involved in a cause they care about. Gruff-looking men will come up to me in airports to say, "I just loved your mother."

**How can you honor the people you love and admire?**

But perhaps the most fitting tribute happened at the Texas capitol, where Mom lay in state for two days before her funeral. Anyone who wanted could come. Former President Bill Clinton was to deliver the eulogy, and while we expected a crowd, we didn't anticipate that thousands of people would travel from far and wide to say farewell, leaving behind handwritten notes, old campaign buttons, and in more than one case, a token from someone who had gotten sober because of her. It was a kind of pilgrimage for farmworkers, teachers, and mothers, who brought their kids to pay their respects to this iconic woman governor.

Today her portrait hangs in the rotunda in Austin. I love seeing the pictures folks take with Mom, who watches over us. For all she accomplished, and all the people she inspired, she left a lot for the rest of us to do. I know that if she were here, she would be at the barricades with us. She'd tell us, *This is it—your only life—so whatever the question, the answer is yes. Don't look back. Don't hesitate.*

# 8

## Resilience

It was a Sunday morning a few years into the job at Planned Parenthood, and I sat in my kitchen in New York drinking coffee with Kirk. The twins were in high school, and I tried to be home on Sundays at least. The 24/7 nature of my work meant there wasn't a lot of extra time for all of us to be together.

The phone rang, and I picked it up. As strange as it is, I can't remember who was on the other end. But I certainly remember what they told me.

"George Tiller has been shot," they said. "He was in his church, handing out programs for the service, when someone came right up and shot him. Reports are he died right there."

I was in shock. "Did they catch the shooter?" I asked.

"Yes, it seems so. He literally just walked up and shot him in front of everyone, in cold blood. This is a terrible, terrible day."

* * *

I have always been an expert worrier, but at Planned Parenthood I'd learned to prioritize the worrying. On any given day the list could begin with "Did we get the website up for the new birth control campaign?" or "What happened in court today in Texas?" But what every Planned Parenthood leader in every state in the country worries about the most is the safety of our staff and patients. On that day in May 2009 our worst fears were realized.

George Tiller was a beloved doctor and an abortion provider in Wichita, Kansas, and while he wasn't a Planned Parenthood doctor, he was an integral part of our community. We referred patients to him, and he to us. For several years he had provided abortions to women from all across the country, particularly women who needed to have an abortion late in their pregnancy. He dealt with some of the most medically complicated cases. The walls of his office were papered with thank-you notes from grateful women he'd treated with dignity and respect at one of the most difficult times of their lives. He had so many sayings, "Tillerisms," as people called them, that someone compiled a list, including: *It is never the wrong time to do the next right thing*, and *It's nice to be important, but it's more important to be nice*. His motto, "Trust women," lives on in buttons and hashtags and is repeated every time pol-

**What does "trust women" mean to you?**

iticians try to intervene in the personal medical decisions of women and their families (which is almost every day).

George was a hero in part because his path was so unlikely. His father was a well-respected women's doctor in Wichita. In the 1950s and '60s, George served in the navy. His plan was to become a dermatologist, until one tragic day, when his sister, brother-in-law, and parents were killed in a plane crash. George decided to go into women's health instead, and before long, women were coming to him to ask, "Can you help us like your father did?" That's when he realized his father had provided abortion care to women in Kansas—something he had never known while his father was alive—and his loss left a void in the community. And so, in the heart of Kansas, a largely conservative Republican state, George became one of the few providers of safe and legal abortion.

Opponents of abortion rights have used threats and violence to try to stop people from providing this care. It's why my home was subject to routine security checks, and it's why Planned Parenthood offers escorts to usher patients inside a center for care, past throngs of sometimes vicious and aggressive protesters. It shouldn't have to take courage for women to get medical care at Planned Parenthood, but often it does. In the years George and his family lived in Wichita, they faced unimaginable threats to their safety. He had been the target of some of the most hateful, violent extremists and had the bullet scars to prove it. One time George was shot in his car by an attacker. She hit his hands, which is the last thing any doctor wants. And another time his clinic was firebombed. Before he began rebuilding, he hung up a sign that said "Hell no, we won't go." The fact that he was in the line of fire every day only made his ability to keep a sense of humor that much more admirable.

He was a gentle man, devoted to his church and family. I had met him at medical conferences and, like others who knew him, appreciated his commitment to the work as well as his passion for politics. He was constantly thinking about the bigger picture and spent a lot of time contemplating how on earth we were going to change the political climate in Kansas, which was hostile to women's reproductive rights. His own favorite Tillerism, and one I often think about to this day, was *Attitude is everything*.

I couldn't believe he was dead. The thought that a terrorist could shoot him in his own church, where he ushered each week, was too much to bear. As I sat there at the kitchen table, I thought of the spree of violent killings of abortion providers back in the 1990s. Until that Sunday morning I had thought—naively—that those days were behind us. It was the first time anything like that had happened in my time as president of Planned Parenthood.

I called Planned Parenthood's CEO in Kansas, Peter Brownlie. Like George, Peter was known across the country for standing up to the state to protect abortion access and the confidentiality of patient medical records. Peter was shaken to his core—George was a friend and a hero, and they had been through so much together.

"Let me know what we can do to support you, Peter," I said. "As soon as you know anything about the service arrangements, can you tell me? So many of us from around the country will want to be there."

Once the funeral was set, I flew out to Kansas. The outpouring of support for George's family—his wife, their four children, and many grandchildren—was overwhelming. "They had to move the service to the biggest church in Wichita," Peter said after my colleague Lynne Randall and I got there. "George's home church couldn't begin to handle the flood of people. Even as it is, they are going to set up overflow space for those who can't make it into the sanctuary."

"I think we need to leave really early tomorrow morning for the service," he went on. "The crowd is going to be enormous, and we have seats, but the protesters are going to be out in force. The local police are expecting Fred Phelps and his group." Phelps and his followers at Westboro Baptist Church in Topeka protested against Catholics, LGBTQ people, the Jewish community, and others. They were notorious for picketing the funerals of military veterans like George, and had been declared a hate group by the Southern Poverty Law Center, which tracks nefarious organizations.

"That sounds right," I replied. "Are you sure you have enough security?"

Peter lifted his shirt. He was wearing a bulletproof vest. "It's what we have to do here in Kansas," he said. There was nothing I could say. That's the kind of courage Planned Parenthood leaders have in states across the country.

The next morning a security car picked us up two hours early, in hopes we could get to the church before the protests got going. It was a clear, quiet morning in Wichita, but as we were coming over the hill near the church, I saw a horde of motorcycles with huge American flags attached to poles off the back. There were dozens lined up, single file, and the riders held their helmets under their arms. I thought to myself, *Oh no, the place is already surrounded by protesters.*

"This doesn't look good," I said to Peter.

The road was open, so we continued on. As we approached, I realized that the motorcyclists weren't there to protest. They were, in fact, the Patriot Guard Riders, a volunteer group that ensures dignity and respect at memorial services honoring military heroes and veterans. As we got out of the car, it was hard not to cry. These burly motorcycle riders were honoring George and protecting his family and friends. We were all Americans, joined in sadness, paying tribute to a fallen hero.

"Thank you," I said as we passed the entourage. "You cannot know what it means to have you here."

"We honor our fellow veterans. It's our duty," one of them replied. Two imposing tattooed men in leather vests quietly escorted George's wife, Jeanne, from her car into the church.

As far as the eye could see, people had gathered to pay tribute to George. Some wore T-shirts with his most famous sayings and held white carnations. Others carried photos of him. The church was full. Out in the lobby, baskets contained Tillerisms written on slips of paper as keepsakes. George was eulogized by his fraternity brothers from the University of Kansas, and his children spoke. The pastor of the church he attended each week was there with an "Attitude Is Everything" button on his robe.

"Just last week," George's daughter Jennifer said, "Dad and I and his grandkids were at Disney World, on every ride. Dad loved it, and I'm so glad we had that time with him. He loved his family."

Jeanne stood up and sang "The Lord's Prayer," which she dedicated "to my best buddy and the love of my life." She has a beautiful voice. I do not know how she was able to get through the song.

Many of our staff and community hadn't been able to go to the services in Kansas, so we planned to have our own memorial for George at our national offices in New York. The word had just gone out that we were holding a service, open to all, when I got a call from Luis Ubiñas, president of the Ford Foundation, one of the most important foundations to support social justice work, including women's rights. Luis and his wife, Deb Tolman, had become friends of mine.

"Deb and I would like to talk at your memorial service for Dr. Tiller," he said.

"Well, that would be wonderful, Luis. We're expecting a lot of people from the community," I replied.

He hesitated for a moment, and I could hear him take a breath on the other end. "But you see," he said, "we especially want to be there, because Dr. Tiller was our doctor."

Deb and Luis have two extraordinary sons, whom I knew. But I hadn't known until that moment that years ago they'd had a much-wanted pregnancy that had come to a heartbreaking end. They had learned late in term that the fetus that had been growing inside Deb was not viable; it would not survive the pregnancy and childbirth. In addition, Deb's life was at risk, and one of only three doctors in the country who could help them was Dr. Tiller. They put their trust in him because he trusted women. As their experience unfolded, they learned that one of the reasons Dr. Tiller was so remarkable was that he loved and respected his patients; he listened to women.

The days surrounding George's death were painfully sad, but they were also a reminder of the incredible power of working with a group of people who can support each other through the most difficult tragedies. There was nothing good to come of all this. A brave man had been shot in cold blood—a man who had cared for so many women, especially women in the most terrible medical circumstances. But George's legacy and work inspired a renewed commitment among many of us. From that day forward, whenever one of us at Planned Parenthood was trying to make an important decision or dealing with the latest political attack, we would ask, *What would George do?* Not long after his death, the Planned Parenthood Federation voted to ensure that every affiliate across the country provided abortion care. The years that followed brought an onslaught of laws introduced in states across the country to make it harder for women to access abortion. As we took on those fights, we returned again and again to George's mantra: "Trust women."

Meanwhile the ground was starting to shift. One of the reasons everyone knew George's name was because he had been public about being an abortion provider. Back then, most were not—and for good reason. In the 1990s,

Dr. David Gunn, Dr. John Britton, and Dr. Barnett Slepian had been murdered, as well as staff at two health centers in Brookline, Massachusetts: Shannon Lowney and Lee Ann Nichols. Extremists targeted abortion providers, practically inviting deadly violence.

After George's death, a wave of doctors began to disrupt the pattern. They understood that we could never change attitudes toward abortion unless people started speaking openly—so that's just what they did. In 2010 the *New York Times Magazine* published a feature story about doctors who provide abortion services, including a brave and committed Planned Parenthood doctor named Rachael Phelps. I was impressed by her courage and knew such a story was breaking new ground. There were plenty of people who felt that speaking out wasn't safe. But because doctors like Dr. Phelps were so brave, more abortion providers are out in the open and more doctors advocate for their patients and for women everywhere—including in the halls of Congress, where they meet with elected officials about the care their patients need. I know George would be proud of these young doctors. Seeing how they're refusing to hide in the shadows fills me with hope that we will one day be able to break out of this political back-and-forth and start recognizing abortion for what it is: health care, and a vital service that is part of so many people's lives.

People often ask, "Why do this? Why get up every day and do work that is so hard?" But the fact is, nobody ever asked the women I worked with in rural Texas, New Orleans, or

East Los Angeles how they got out of bed every morning to do their tough jobs cleaning hotel rooms and caring for the elderly. Being able to choose to do work that makes a difference is a privilege. When you're working for social change, there are new battles every day, and you never know if you're going to lose or win. But when I go home at night, if I can look in the mirror and say, *I did the right thing by women*, that's what matters.

When another awful bill is introduced in another state legislature to limit women's health care options, or I'm trying to counter lies about Planned Parenthood on national television, I often think of the health center manager I met in Des Moines, Iowa. One morning, before the center opened, we talked while she set up her procedure room for the day, organizing the cabinets the way she liked and getting the exam table ready for the first patient.

> **Can you think of anyone you know who works really hard? How are they making a difference?**

"You know," she confessed, "it gets hard, especially with the politics and the protesters. A few months ago I even started thinking about taking an easier job. But then I came to work, and I saw my patients. I held a woman's hand through her procedure and looked her in the eye. And I realized: they need me. They need me as much as any person has ever needed someone. How can I walk out on them?" She's right. At the end of the day, that's all that matters.

Of course that doesn't make it any more fun to listen to the things people yell at me when I walk into a health center, or to read what people say about me on Twitter (something I try to avoid at all costs). Worst of all are the awful things people say about my kids—those really hurt.

I try never to totally shut out criticism—after all, sometimes there's a grain of truth to it. But I've learned from Mom's experiences and my own not to let it determine how I feel about myself. If I did, I simply would not be able to function some days—like the time, in the middle of an effort to defund Planned Parenthood, when my personal email address wound up on an antiabortion blog. In a matter of hours my inbox was full of the same hateful message copied and pasted from thousands of people, telling me I was a baby killer, I was going to hell, and all the rest. More than anything else, it was profoundly annoying having to dig through all the junk in order to find the emails I actually needed to read.

But then, by accident or by chance, I opened one of the emails. It began, "I know you think this is just going to be another awful screed against you and against Planned Parenthood. Your email address was forwarded to me from my mother-in-law, who sent it to all of her antichoice friends. I'm hoping somehow you find this note among all the hate mail because I think Planned Parenthood is great. You were there for me when I was in college, and I'll never forget it." Right there, in the middle of it all, was a diamond in the rough. That's true most of the time, if you're willing to look for it.

Every job has its own hurdles and challenges, and doing the right work means there will be some tough days. If

there aren't, I figure I need to set my sights
higher. Some of them have left me sad
and resolute, while others have helped me
reconnect to the core of why I do what I do.
And knowing that there are people who get

**How do you
intend to be "in
the fight"?**

up every day, face down the picketers and protesters, and
do everything they can to help a woman with a lump in her
breast or a young couple get the health care they deserve is
what makes me want to stay in the fight.

## If It Was Easy, Someone Else
## Would Be Doing It

Molly Ivins, who was a feisty Texas newspaper columnist and a friend of my family, said it best: "Since you don't always win, you got to learn to enjoy just fightin' the good fight."

In all my years as an organizer, I've learned that you lose a lot more than you win. If you can't celebrate the victories when they come along, and have a little fun the rest of the time, you just might be in the wrong line of work.

To put this in context: When Planned Parenthood was founded more than a hundred years ago, birth control was illegal. Back in 1916 a nurse named Margaret Sanger, along with her sister Ethel and a volunteer named Fania Mindell, opened the first birth control clinic in America. It was a tiny storefront in Brooklyn, New York, where women could get a ten-cent pamphlet about preventing pregnancy. From day one women lined up around the block—women pushing baby buggies, holding babies in their arms. Ten days later an undercover police officer posing as a mother busted Margaret and threw her in jail—where she taught her fellow inmates about birth control.

Margaret began traveling the country, and a movement was born. She spoke to nurses in St. Paul, Minnesota, and women's clubs in Los Angeles; factory women in Racine, Wisconsin, and farmworkers in Tucson, Arizona. When the city council of Portland, Oregon, met behind closed doors to ban Margaret's pamphlets, the women in town made pamphlets of their own, which read, "Shall five men legislate in secret against ten thousand women?" Suddenly Planned Parenthood centers started cropping up in towns across America. Once, on a visit to Dallas, I stopped by the Ripley Shirt Factory. Years ago Katie Ripley, with the full knowledge of her husband, George, who owned the factory, would send empty shirt boxes to New York City. Organizers there would fill them with diaphragms, one of the earliest types of birth control, mark them "Returns," and ship them back to Dallas, where women would gratefully get them. It wasn't until the 1960s that a Planned Parenthood employee in Connecticut named Estelle Griswold decided to challenge the laws outlawing birth control. With the help of her medical director, Dr. C. Lee Buxton, she started handing out birth control to women in hopes of getting arrested. And after the police did indeed arrest her, Estelle fought her case all the way to the US Supreme Court. In 1965 *Griswold v. Connecticut* legalized birth control for married couples.

Women have been searching for ways to prevent pregnancy for all of recorded history. In the United States we've been fighting about women's reproductive rights for the better part of the past century, and there's no sign of that changing anytime soon. All these conflicts bubbled up to the surface in the struggle to reform our complex and inadequate health insurance system.

When you go to the doctor, you probably don't think about how the doctors get paid or who buys high-tech machines to test your blood or x-ray your bones. But medical care is expensive, and many Americans have health insurance to help cover the costs of it. They pay a monthly bill, called a premium, to have a health insurance policy, and then a copay—sometimes twenty or thirty or fifty dollars—each time they see a doctor or have a medical procedure. This means when you get sick, you can see a doctor and get the tests or medications or surgeries he or she thinks you need and not pay too much, even though the procedures are costly. Most grown-ups get health insurance for their families through their jobs.

But what happens if your job doesn't provide health insurance? Over the course of the last few decades, fewer and fewer Americans have been offered health insurance at their jobs. And what if you lose your job? You and your family lose your health insurance. Then if any of you get sick, your family is in big trouble. Not only do you not have insurance to help cover the costs of health care, but you also don't have any income to pay for the doctors' visits, tests, surgeries, and medicine.

Passing health reform had been one of President Obama's signature campaign promises, and he made it a top priority soon after taking office in 2009. Back then, nearly 50 million Americans had no insurance. At Planned Parenthood we saw patients every day who couldn't afford medical treatment because they lacked health insurance. When President Obama unveiled the Affordable Care Act—also known as Obamacare—it was an amazing opportunity to take a big leap forward.

In the early days of the fight for health care reform, I went to an event with Barbara Mikulski, a senator from Maryland and the longest-serving woman in Congress, to announce Planned Parenthood's support for Obamacare. She jumped up to the microphone and pulled out her bright red lipstick. Smearing it on, she shouted, "Get ready, women, we are going to war!"

Of course she was right. During the many months it took to pass Obamacare, one question came up again and again: Should Obamacare health insurance plans include coverage for women's reproductive health care? That would mean insurance would cover care for pregnant women, women giving birth, gynecological exams, and breast cancer screenings. In one infamous hearing, Republican Senator Jon Kyl from Arizona objected to covering maternity care for pregnant women, huffing, "I've never needed it." Senator Debbie Stabenow of Michigan shot back, "I think your mother probably did." Such debates shined a spotlight on the absurdity of these questions. Women's health care isn't some special perk; it's fundamental to the lives of anyone who has ever had or been a mother, sister, daughter, aunt, wife, or grandmother—in other words, everyone.

After many similar arguments had been waged and won, there was one last topic to resolve: the issue of abortion. An amendment to the bill had been introduced at the last minute that would prevent insurance plans from covering abortion services under the new health care law. The proposal, called the Stupak Amendment (its sponsor was Congressman Bart Stupak), went against everything we stood for at Planned Parenthood.

When the House of Representatives voted, the Stupak Amendment passed. If the bill including the amendment passed the Senate, it would then head to the president's desk for his signature and would become law. We'd lose abortion coverage for women and never get it back. I was devastated. It was my lowest point in a long time.

Early the next morning I was in a hotel room, getting ready for a day on the road, when my cell phone rang. My old boss, Nancy Pelosi, was calling. At this time, the Democrats held the majority in both houses of Congress—the House of Representatives and the Senate. Nancy Pelosi was the powerful Speaker of the House, the leader of the House Democrats. "I know this is terrible, and I'm as mad as you are," she said. "This was a last-minute attack and just know this: I am committed to getting the Stupak Amendment out of the final bill. I don't know how, but that's my word."

I thanked her and told her we would help however we could. But I wasn't hopeful. Having worked in Congress, I knew it would be nearly impossible. And deep down I knew that the White House would sign whatever bill came out of Congress. We couldn't count on the president to veto the bill everyone in his administration had fought so hard for. I felt awful and totally discouraged.

A few days later Planned Parenthood leaders from across the country were scheduled to be in Washington for a meeting of the national board. Everyone was expecting an update from the front lines of the health care fight. Our organization had poured all our energy into supporting Obamacare, and there was so much good in the bill. But I knew we could not support it the way it was. I just hoped the board would agree.

"This is it," I told them, bracing for a tough conversation. "I am asking you to give me the authority to tell the White House and our congressional leaders that if the bill bans abortion coverage, as it does in its current version, we will lobby against final passage."

There was an uneasy silence. For months, our volunteers had rallied, made phone calls, and come to Washington to speak to their members of Congress—all in the interest of getting Obamacare passed. To see those efforts derailed would be awful. I could sense the board members thinking, *All this work, for nothing?*

The board went back and forth. When you're sick, you depend on your doctor's guidance about how best to be healthy. But when it comes to women's reproductive health care, politicians always seem to think they know better than you and your doctor. There was no way we could support a bill that would tie the hands of doctors and patients, limit their options. But if Planned Parenthood opposed Obamacare over abortion, the entire bill might go down, hurting the millions of Americans in desperate need of affordable health care.

In the middle of our discussion, Reverend Kelvin Sauls, a board member and preacher from California, cleared his throat. He had a forceful voice and everyone in the board-room stopped their conversations and leaned forward to listen. "The Bible says, 'And I sought for a man among them, that should stand in the breach before me.' The question we must answer is, Who will stand in the breach? Who will stand for the women we care for, at a moment of need for moral leadership? I believe this is one of those times when we are called to be in solidarity with women who may have no one else to stand in the breach." When he finished speaking, the room erupted with applause. Reverend Sauls had put into words what everyone was feeling. The board voted unanimously that Planned Parenthood would not support the bill if it banned abortion coverage—even if that meant the defeat of the very bill we had worked so hard for.

> **Have you ever stood up for someone in need, even when it wasn't popular to do so? Did you ever wish you had when you didn't?**

It was my job to deliver the message. First I had to call the White House, knowing that they would be furious. I had to remember what the president told me and other activists after he was first elected: "It's your job to make me do the right thing." That sounded good as a slogan, but the reality was that no one liked being pressured by us.

Our only real hope was Speaker Pelosi, and though I

remembered her pledge to me weeks earlier, her opposing this bill, here at the final hour, seemed nearly impossible. I knew how important health care reform was to her, and to millions of Americans. Our position wasn't popular enough to defeat the entire bill. But I needed to tell her where Planned Parenthood stood, and I needed to tell her directly.

Waiting at the Capitol for my appointment with Nancy, I saw everyone I had ever worked with on the Hill—it was like a slightly awkward family reunion. I was wearing my best blue suit, with a pin of Mom's that looked like a sheriff's badge. I was going to need her help from on high that day.

Being ushered into the conference room was a good reminder of how very different it was to be on the other side of the table from my former boss. This wasn't a negotiating meeting; I knew I had to be crystal clear on our position, take it or leave it.

"Thanks for coming in today," Nancy began. "I know you understand we are within only a handful of votes to get this bill passed, and I'm not sure we can get it done. But we are working hard."

That wasn't surprising to me, since everyone was hustling votes and it was down to the wire. But then, before I had a chance to make my case, she floored me.

"You know how much this bill means to me. I've worked for health care reform my entire career," Speaker Pelosi said. "But I want you to know: if there is an abortion ban in the Affordable Care Act, there won't be an Affordable Care Act. I won't pass it."

I opened my mouth to thank her, but once again Nancy

was a step ahead of me, already strategizing on how to get the caucus (the other Democrats in Congress) in line. Her deputies—other members of the Democratic congressional leadership—were hard at work trying to convince other Democratic members of Congress to vote for it. Soon we would know whether the abortion ban had made it into the final bill—not to mention whether the bill could even pass.

That whole week was an endless vote-counting effort, and time on the congressional calendar was running out. Soon the voting would be over, for better or worse. We had Planned Parenthood supporters calling every member of Congress, either to thank them for their support or urge them to support only a bill that protected abortion rights.

At the end of the week my phone rang. It was Congresswoman Rosa DeLauro from Connecticut. She worked closely with Speaker Pelosi and had never shied away from a fight.

"Cecile, we did it! We backed them down. They threatened us over and over," Rosa said. "And it won't surprise you—several of the Democratic men were ready to sell us out. But Nancy didn't blink. None of the women blinked. The Stupak abortion ban is out of the bill!"

Joy and relief washed over me, along with an overwhelming feeling of gratitude for the women who had stood with us. It was amazing. Had we really done this?

Yes, we had. Two days later the Affordable Care Act passed with no Stupak Amendment, and we made history. Without the women in the House and the Senate, it would have been a different story. Starting with Senator Mikulski, who announced that we were going to war, women in Congress were key to every victory for women under Obamacare. And of course, they were aided in their efforts by women from around the country who spoke out and told their stories.

For the first time, insurance companies could no longer charge women more than men for the same health care coverage—something that routinely happened before Obamacare. And companies could not deny insurance coverage to women if they were pregnant or had been abused in the past, which insurers had done before the law passed.

Protecting coverage for abortion was a major victory, but certainly not our last battle in the fight for women's health care. Health insurance also helps pay for medications, and we wanted to make sure birth control was covered under Obamacare. Planned Parenthood saw more than two million patients for birth control each year, but what we were talking about could be life-changing for tens of millions of women.

There are three things to know about birth control. First, it's incredibly popular; more than 90 percent of women will use it at some point. Second, too often women don't use the birth control method that's best for them because they can't afford it. Third, a lot of people (58 percent of women using birth control, to be precise) rely on birth control at least in part for reasons other than preventing pregnancy, such as treating acne, cramps, or endometriosis, a painful disorder of the reproductive system. Others use it because they want to be able to have sex and not get pregnant—also a compelling reason! The bottom line? Birth control is basic health care for millions of people.

Most people agree. Opponents might want to pretend that isn't true, but ignoring reality and facts doesn't help anyone. And yet standing in the way of health care coverage for birth control were some very high-ranking challengers, including the Conference of Catholic Bishops and the Catholic Hospital Association. And so we revved up our supporters once again to fight. Could we win this battle too?

One morning in February 2012, I was sitting in our office in Washington, when my phone rang. The woman on the other end said, "Would you please hold for the president of the United States?"

"I can definitely do that," I said, thinking, *This is the first time in my life I've gotten a call from the president of the United States. Whatever he says, at least I'll always have that!*

A minute later President Obama—who is famous for being on time—came to the phone. "Hey, Cecile, how's it going?" he asked in a cheerful voice.

"Well, hello, Mr. President. It's going just fine, thanks."

"Cecile, I wanted to call you because I'm making three phone calls today: the Catholic Bishops, the Catholic Hospital Association, and you. Suffice it to say, I think yours is going to be the happiest phone call I'm going to make."

At that point I started feeling hopeful.

"I'm going to tell them the same thing I'm telling you: later today, I'm going to announce at the White House that, from here on out, birth control is going to be covered for all women under their insurance plans with no copay. I know you've worked hard for this, and I think it's going to be a huge advance for women."

I took a deep breath. "Well, Mr. President, thank you for calling me yourself, and for understanding what a difference this is going to make. We're going to be busy making sure women know about this benefit and can get it."

Later, the entire staff gathered around a television in a conference room to watch as the president took the podium in the White House press briefing room to announce publicly what he'd told me over the phone.

"Whether you're a teacher, or a small businesswoman, or a nurse, or a janitor, no woman's health should depend on who she is or where she works or how much money she makes. Every woman should be in control of the decisions that affect her own health. Period."

We let out a cheer. It was a phenomenal moment, surrounded by Planned Parenthood staff who had spent months organizing, tweeting, writing reports, and gathering the stories of women across the country. We hugged, high-fived, and took it all in for a few minutes. Then we started strategizing about what we needed to do to make sure birth control with no copay was a rousing success.

And it was. As soon as the birth control benefit took effect, women started walking into pharmacies to refill their prescriptions, walking out with another month's supply of birth control without having to pay a dime. They'd go to check out at the doctor's office after a well-woman exam, ask what they owed, and hear the receptionist say, "The total for your visit is zero dollars." Women started sending Planned

Parenthood thank-you notes written on the back of a Walgreens receipt, with the copay circled: $0.00.

Here's the headline: In the first year alone, women saved $1.4 billion on birth control pills. Today we're at a thirty-year low for unintended pregnancy, a historic low in teen pregnancy, and the lowest abortion rate since the *Roe v. Wade* decision forty-five years ago. These facts are too often overlooked, even though this is one of the biggest public health success stories of the last century. It didn't happen on its own—it happened in large part due to better and more affordable access to birth control.

But of course elections have consequences. Since President Obama left office, women's health has come under fire by the Trump administration, which believes insurance companies shouldn't have to cover birth control. While the Obama administration was full of people—including the president himself—who were aware of how many women rely on affordable birth control, the current administration is home to high-ranking officials who claim it doesn't work and don't think it should have to be covered by insurance.

**How can you spread the truth about women's reproductive health?**

At a time when so many people's opinions on issues of reproductive health seem to be set in stone, it can seem nearly impossible to change someone's mind. By refusing to back down on birth control coverage in the Affordable Care Act, we certainly changed the way a lot of people understood birth control. Men who once rolled their eyes when they heard about it were persuaded by women from all walks of life who felt so strongly about making their own health care choices.

There is a message here for aspiring troublemakers: we get only what we're willing to fight for—nothing more and, I hope, nothing less. That's a lesson I learned growing up in Texas. During the summer of 2013, the rest of the country learned a little something about it too.

It started when Texas governor Rick Perry and the state legislature shut down the women's health program in the state, closing more than eighty health centers, the vast majority of which were not even run by Planned Parenthood. All were health care providers that delivered basic medical care to folks who didn't have the money to be able to go to just any doctor or who couldn't travel long distances for care.

In a fervent effort to get rid of Planned Parenthood, they tried to force through laws that would essentially end access to safe and legal abortion. The measures they were trying to pass would close all but five of the remaining abortion clinics left in the state, which is a big deal in a state as geographically huge as Texas.

By that point, women in Texas had been so beat down that the governor and his friends must have thought they would be too exhausted to fight back. Instead it was like a match on dry kindling. Suddenly Texans from every corner of the state were showing up to testify against the bills. Parents left kids with neighbors and headed to the capitol.

Students from colleges all over the state drove to Austin to stand in line for the chance to get their three minutes before the Texas Senate to oppose the legislation. Hundreds of activists waited for hours, some until two or three in the morning. People in California and Wisconsin watching on social media ordered pizza and coffee to be delivered to protesters at the capitol.

Legislation terrible for women was being debated in states across the country, but Texas was clearly in a class all its own. I had been doing this work a long time, but I had never seen spontaneous organizing like this.

I was on a train when I got a call from Kirk Watson, the former mayor of Austin, a longtime friend, and now a Texas state senator and head of the Democratic caucus in the state legislature. "Look, this bill's happening," he told me. "I know we don't have the votes to block it. We can't win. But I think we can filibuster the bill. This is our chance to say something."

To filibuster, a state senator would have to talk until they ran out the clock—actually stand and talk for thirteen hours with no breaks and no rest, not even to sit briefly. There was a time limit on the bill. After midnight, the legislature wouldn't be able to vote on it, and then the bill would die. The Democrats had someone lined up to do it: Senator Wendy Davis from Fort Worth.

I got to Austin in time to see Wendy lacing up her now-famous pink running shoes, and I could see the determination in her eyes: she was definitely ready. On the front door of her office she'd hung a sign reading "Stand with

Planned Parenthood." As she explained, "I want to make sure every senator has to walk by this sign on their way to the floor."

The energy in Austin that day was like nothing I'd ever experienced. The line to get into the senate to watch Wendy's filibuster snaked up three stories of the capitol rotunda, and every overflow room was full to capacity. And lots of people brought their kids—reproductive rights are a family affair!

As I walked around, taking it all in, I met a seven-year-old activist named Scarlett who had set up shop in a corner of the capitol, where she was decorating and distributing homemade pins that said, "Stand with Wendy." I still have mine.

At 11:18 a.m. the filibuster started. Wendy stood up, her posture strong and defiant, and said, "I intend to speak for an extended length of time." She read facts about abortion, testimony from Planned Parenthood doctors and patients. Every time I started to worry she might be losing steam, she launched into another powerful personal account from yet another woman in Texas. It was as if the struggles of those women boosted her, reminding her of what we were fighting for, and kept her knees from buckling. She'd have to keep going until midnight.

But that didn't stop Lieutenant Governor David Dewhurst, who was also president of the senate, from trying to halt the filibuster by any means necessary before midnight—even if it meant breaking every rule in the book to do it. I was with the crowd outside the chamber where Wendy was speaking and I realized that if they cut Wendy off, the capitol was going to erupt. That's when I turned to Earl Jordan, the head of security for Planned Parenthood of Greater Texas.

"Earl," I said, "if they declare the filibuster dead, we're going to jail tonight. So I need you to get ready."

Earl didn't miss a beat. "No, ma'am. No, ma'am, we're not," he said in his calm drawl. Translation: *Don't even think about trying something.*

I just looked at him. There were thousands of people in the capitol, and it was clear to me that we were going to have a massive protest if they tried to end Wendy's filibuster. People would simply refuse to budge and they would get arrested. And I was convinced that was what we needed. No one was going to be able to change my mind, not even Earl. I began to look around the rotunda for lawyers I knew and texted a few others who could be on call in case we all went to jail. Then I turned to the women on either side of me. "Now might be a good time to put your ID in your bra. That way you'll have it if we get arrested later." I'd learned a few things since my first arrest back in California.

Meanwhile, back inside the chambers, Republicans had not only stopped Wendy's filibuster and tried to call a vote, but they had cut off the microphones on the Democratic side. It was complete chaos.

I was standing out in the rotunda, surrounded by people chanting, and by cameras clicking, when I got a text message from someone inside the chamber on the senate floor. It just said, "Make noise." And so we did. We shook the capitol to its foundation. We knew that our last hope of stopping the bill before midnight was to create so much raucous noise and chaos that they couldn't continue with business as usual. The lieutenant governor called us an "unruly mob." Funny—in some parts of the world, they call that democracy in action.

We continued to rally well past midnight. The Department of Public Safety threw everyone out of the senate gallery, but nobody left the capitol. At one point the Republican leadership in the state legislature even tried to change the clock on the senate floor to make it look like they had passed the bill in time. They were trying to claim the filibuster had failed.

Finally, around three a.m., we got the news: the bill was dead. Wendy's filibuster had worked!

Democracy in action.

In the midst of the deafening applause, I kept looking up at Mom's portrait in the rotunda. She ran for governor to open up the doors of government and let the people in, and here we were. She would have been so proud. There was nothing she loved better than making good trouble. I had to make a plane back to New York at daybreak, but it was four a.m. and I was starving, so Earl and I drove to the only place open for breakfast at that hour, an all-night diner packed full of Planned Parenthood supporters.

We wedged in with the rest of the protesters and celebrated with a stack of pancakes.

Within days, we got the news that Governor Perry had called a second special legislative session to pass the bill. We knew it was coming, and we knew we had to keep people organized and our fight in the news. So we got to work planning a statewide bus tour and headed out on orange buses emblazoned with "Stand with Texas Women." The two buses (nicknamed "Ann" after Mom and "Maggie" after Margaret Sanger) crisscrossed the state, greeted by crowds in Houston, Dallas, San Antonio, and even in smaller, more conservative towns like Midland in West Texas. Everywhere she went, Wendy Davis got a hero's welcome. Women would walk up to me with tears in their eyes and share deeply personal stories about ending a pregnancy while struggling with medically unnecessary laws intended to shame them. No matter the outcome of our fight, they were determined to stand up and be counted.

Days later, when the bill came up for a vote, we didn't

have the votes to block it, nor could we filibuster again. Even so, people were still showing up in droves.

Walking up the steps to the capitol that morning, feeling somber but determined, I passed a mother and her young son. The mom elbowed him, saying, "Show her your sign." He held up a piece of orange poster board on which he had written in Magic Marker, "I still have my mom thanks to cancer screenings at Planned Parenthood." His mother started to cry and said simply, "Thank you." I gave them both a hug and went into the capitol.

As usual, everyone had to go through security. But this time the Department of Public Safety was confiscating women's tampons and sanitary napkins, apparently worried that the women would throw them from the gallery onto the senate floor. Senator Kirk Watson joked, "I'm really confused—I thought sanitary napkins were kind of soft, fluffy things." It was irony at its finest: you could bring a gun into the state capitol, but not a tampon.

That night, after the bill passed, we held a rally and marched past the governor's mansion carrying a sign that read, "In it for the long run!"

Later, when I went to bed, I couldn't sleep. All I could think of were the people I'd met and the makeshift family we had built. There were activists of all ages who had been part of this—including one of my favorites, Beau Guidry. At nine years old, Beau had not only watched every minute of Wendy Davis's filibuster, but he had live-tweeted it. Later that fall he would run for president of his third-grade class—and win.

* * *

The best and worst part about being a professional troublemaker is that the trouble never ends. Once the law we'd been protesting took effect, we had to continue fighting back while making sure women could still get abortions in Texas, despite the unbelievable barriers they faced. And we had to make sure we told these women's stories.

Women who were scheduled to have an abortion on Friday morning showed up and found out it had been canceled. One woman who came to Planned Parenthood was stricken. "What do you mean, I have to come back? I can't. I've left my kids with my neighbor and can't miss another day of work." She left, sobbing, and never returned.

One of the many heroines from those awful days is Melaney Linton, a Planned Parenthood CEO who oversees parts of Texas and Louisiana. The day after the law took effect, and other abortion providers were forced to close their doors, Melaney reported that her staff was working around the clock to be there for the flood of patients who filled their waiting room, lobby, patio, hallway, and parking lot. "We are still providing services," she said. "We will never, ever go down without a fight."

We knew the law would eventually make its way to the Supreme Court, which would rule whether or not it was constitutional (we were certain it wasn't). I was honored to be in the courtroom to watch oral arguments before the court. And for the first time in American history, three women served on the bench—Justices Ruth Bader Ginsburg, Elena Kagan, and Sonia Sotomayor—thanks to President Obama's appointment of Justices Kagan and Sotomayor.

The irony of that day's argument? The lawyer for the state of Texas couldn't give a single reason why enacting these restrictions was for the benefit of women. Minutes into the lawyer's oral argument, Justice Ginsburg set the tone for the hearing by asking how many women lived one hundred miles or more from a clinic under the new law. He answered that it would be about 25 percent, but that didn't include women in El Paso, who could go to the clinic just over the border in New Mexico. At that, Justice Ginsburg sat up straighter.

"That's odd that you point to the New Mexico facility," she asserted, referring to the fact that New Mexico doesn't require clinics to meet the difficult and unnecessary requirements Texas claimed were so important to protect women's health and safety. "If that's all right for the women in the El Paso area, why isn't it right for the rest of the women in Texas?" It was a knockout punch.

It wasn't simply that the women justices dominated the argument and had read every page of the material. They were able to bring something that had seldom been heard before in the Supreme Court: women's lives and experiences. It was proof that elections matter, because elected officials decide who sits on the court: the president nominates a justice to the Supreme Court, and that choice must be approved by the Senate. Those three women on the court, twenty-two others in the US Senate, and many more in the US House of Representatives are carrying all of us on their shoulders.

Months later, on the day of the verdict, the Supreme Court had ruled 5–3 against the Texas law, with Justice Ginsburg noting that it was "beyond rational belief" that the law "could genuinely protect the health of women." I couldn't have put it better!

Of course the fight is far from over, and women in Texas are still living with enormous barriers. But not long ago Planned Parenthood started providing abortions again in my hometown of Waco, an important sign of hope and progress.

Mom used to quote the poet Edna St. Vincent Millay, who said, "It's not true that life is one damn thing after another; it's one damn thing over and over."

Abortion was legalized by the Supreme Court more than four decades ago, and extreme politicians have been chipping away at a woman's right to make her own health decisions ever since. In fact, we've seen more attempts in the past five years than ever before to make it harder to access safe and legal abortion. I often think of the signs I see at protests for reproductive rights, typically held by older women, reading, "My arms are tired from carrying this sign for 40 years."

**What does it mean to you to have control over your body?**

You may be wondering—what is all the fuss about? And why do women feel so strongly about maintaining their right to abortion? At its heart, what these activists—from Margaret Sanger to Nancy Pelosi to Melaney Linton to millions of others—are fighting for is the right to make decisions about our bodies that are best for us. Full stop.

Four years ago I started speaking more publicly about my own abortion. Before becoming president of Planned Parenthood, I hadn't talked about it except to family and close friends. The truth is, it wasn't an agonizing decision for me. It wasn't tragic or dramatic—it was just my story.

Kirk and I were working more than full-time and had three kids in school when I realized I was pregnant again. Like millions of other women, I was using birth control, but birth control sometimes fails. We were doing the best job we could raising our kids, and I couldn't imagine we could do a good job for a fourth child. Having another child just was not an option for us. I already felt like I wasn't doing enough for Lily, Hannah, and Daniel as it was. I was fortunate in that, at the time, getting an abortion in Texas was not the nightmare it now is for so many women.

Being able to terminate a pregnancy early—it had hardly even begun—was a relief. I realize women have many different feelings about abortion, and I respect that. But the thought that the government could force me or any other woman to carry out a pregnancy that was unplanned or unwanted was and is absolutely wrong. Many women have echoed how I feel. And the truth is, without safe and legal abortions, women will find other ways to end pregnancies—through methods that are dangerous to their health, even deadly. It's also why we offer sex education to teens and lots of birth control options—if people are going to have sex (and they will!), let's make sure it's safe and healthy.

After my public declaration, women came up to me from Arizona to Maine to tell me that they had decided to share their stories too.

In 2016 I was at a conference celebrating 125 years of women students at Brown University, my alma mater. I was sitting in the audience, making last-minute edits to my speech, when a middle-aged woman took the stage to introduce me. Something in her voice made me sit up and pay attention.

She thanked Brown and gave a shout-out to her daughter, who was in the audience. Then she started to tell her own story. Days before her graduation in 1968, she traveled to Philadelphia for an illegal abortion. A few days later, barely able to stand, she got out of bed and welcomed her parents to campus. She managed to walk through the campus gates to get her diploma, hiding how much pain she was in.

Looking back, she said, she was lucky to be alive. She choked up as she said she would not be where she is today had she not been able to get an abortion. "We can't ever go back," she insisted. It was the first time she had ever told her story in public.

We're still waging the fight for abortion access in America every day. But along the way we're also transforming the culture, and that change can't be reversed.

It's a controversial issue, where both sides have strong feelings, and taking on controversial issues is hard. Since my first weeks at Planned Parenthood, there have been people who have said, "Why don't you just change the name, or split the organization in two, so people don't associate you with abortion?" Sometimes these are well-intentioned people; they just want the controversy to go away. But what is important is that we quit apologizing for abortion and do everything we can to support people who need one.

Anytime you're trying to change the way things are or challenge the powers that be, it's going to be controversial. That's been true in every organizing job I've ever had. Often the work that's most worthwhile seems the most stubborn and impossible. But just because someone else hasn't figured it out yet doesn't mean you can't. After all, if it was easy, someone else would be doing it. And in the meantime, at least I'm enjoying fighting the good fight.

# 10

## Don't Let the Bastards Get You Down

Sometimes the good fight comes looking for you. That was certainly the case when I had to testify before a congressional committee in 2015. Members of Congress hold hearings for many reasons: to get expert testimony on a proposed law, to question government agencies that they oversee, or to investigate wrongdoing. The purpose of this hearing was, at least in theory, to examine whether Planned Parenthood had done something really bad. That question was being hotly debated across America since antiabortion activists released a series of misleading videos claiming that our organization sold fetal tissue, which, of course, was not true. Congressional Republicans were using the attack to launch their latest assault on Planned Parenthood. Some had even threatened to shut down the government unless our funding was cut.

There is a mistaken idea that the government sends a blank check to Planned Parenthood to perform abortions. Totally false. First, it's against the law for government to fund most abortions, so those services are kept separate in our books. Second, most of the money Planned Parenthood gets from the government is to pay for preventive services for women on Medicaid—remember, that's the government program that pays for medical care for people who can't afford health insurance. But the facts have never stopped opponents of women's health and women's rights from spoiling for a fight.

And so, on September 29, 2015, it was my responsibility to set the record straight. The congressional hearing room on Capitol Hill was packed with Planned Parenthood staff and supporters and with antiabortion activists, who looked like the same people who stood outside our health centers on Saturday mornings, trying to intimidate patients with graphic pictures on huge poster boards and signs with gruesome, threatening slogans. The kinds of people who wrote me letters that said, "I wish your mother had aborted you." Taking my seat at a large table at the front of the hearing room, I could feel them behind me in the gallery, their hostility radiating through the room.

On the other side of the table were dozens of members of the press corps, nearly all men, with blank expressions and their cameras pointing at me. I was used to the crazy opposition; the rest, not so much.

I poured myself a glass of water and looked around the room, trying to focus on the people and not the bright TV lights or the constant click of cameras. It helped to know that my team was there, along with throngs of supporters in pink T-shirts in the hearing room and lining the hallways outside.

Congresswoman Carolyn Maloney had waved to me as I sat down, and Sheila Jackson Lee, a congresswoman from my home state of Texas who wasn't even on the committee, was sitting there in solidarity. I reminded myself that across the country, hundreds of "Stand with Planned Parenthood" rallies were happening. I was by myself at the table, but I definitely wasn't alone in the fight. Besides, I had a mission to accomplish that was bigger than me. I had prepared well—it was too important not to. My secret weapon? Taped on the inside flap of my massive binder was a photograph of my three kids taken years ago, when they were toddlers. If the hearing got heated—as I assumed it would—I could sneak a peek and remember my support system. I hoped they would help get me through anything headed my way, as they had more than once before.

At ten a.m. Congressman Jason Chaffetz rapped his gavel on the table in front of him and called the committee to order.

He launched into an emotional opening statement, talking about women in his life and their experiences with cancer, and the fact that his wife was working for a plastic surgeon whose patients were breast cancer survivors. Then the mudslinging began.

He didn't mention the 320,000 breast exams Planned Parenthood provides to women each year, or the fact that if Planned Parenthood were defunded, many of those women would have nowhere else to go. It was clear there wasn't going to be any fact-finding; he already had the "facts" he wanted.

The loads of documents we provided to Congress ahead of the hearing had already made it clear that Planned Parenthood had not done anything wrong. So if I was going to go through this exercise, I was going to use my time in front of the committee to talk about the incredible health care women get at Planned Parenthood centers across the country every day and to be a voice for our doctors, staff, and patients. I was not about to let them down.

Two months earlier, on July 14, 2015, I woke up to an email from Planned Parenthood's vice president of communications, Eric Ferrero. He wanted to let me know about a new, heavily edited "undercover" video that had been released by a group calling itself the Center for Medical Progress. The video made it look as if Planned Parenthood doctors and staff were talking callously about selling fetal tissue. Despite the name of the group, they were not a center, and they definitely weren't for medical progress; they were just another offshoot of the same right-wing antiabortion leaders who had been trying to tear down our organization for years.

We had been through video scams before, but this was much more detailed than anything we'd ever seen. They had spent tens of thousands of dollars creating a fake website and building a fake organization. They had posed as representatives of a biotechnology company and, equipped with spy cameras, asked leading questions of Planned Parenthood doctors and staff while they secretly recorded them.

The videos were on every news channel. The next day's headline in the *New York Times* read, "Video Accuses Planned Parenthood of Crime." Politicians seized the opportunity to pile on. We had been the victim of an elaborate hoax—one coordinated between these antiabortion zealots and certain Republican members of Congress. We were under attack.

My first concern was for our patients and for our staff who had been the unknowing victims of the video campaign. If what was happening was awful for the rest of us, it was even worse for the staff members. Patients were counting on them every day.

> This video was "fake news." How do you know what's fake and what's real online?

I will never forget the people who called me in solidarity—and there were many. To balance out the calls from reporters and the anger I felt about what had happened, I tore off a sheet from a gigantic roll of paper and taped it to the wall of my office in Washington. Every time someone called to offer help, I wrote down their name. The early calls came from all over. By the end of the first week, there were so many names on the list I had to add more sheets, until the wall was completely covered. It was an important way to remind my staff and myself of the outpouring of love and support for Planned Parenthood at such a terrifying time.

For the rest of the summer and into the fall we were living in a state of fear and uncertainty; it was almost like dealing with kidnappers. I'd wake up every morning not knowing what was coming, while the group continued releasing more falsified footage.

Everyone at Planned Parenthood felt incredibly vulnerable, knowing our opponents were trying to sneak into the organization to hurt us. There were people out there with hidden cameras, trying to entrap our staff, "befriend" them, or even get a job at Planned Parenthood—all for the purpose of shutting us down.

Folks dug deep to find ways to stay focused and sane, and I was no exception. I had a hard time sleeping and felt even worse knowing how worried my kids were about me. I could understand; I had felt the same way years earlier watching my own mother endure brutal political attacks as governor of Texas.

As we dealt with the constant battering, Republicans in Congress held vote after vote to try to block Medicaid patients from being able to come to Planned Parenthood for preventive care, like a regular checkup visit with their Planned Parenthood doctor.

In the weeks leading up to the hearing, I worked with my team to prepare. The key to this hearing was knowing every fact inside and out, but also telling the stories of the women whose lives and futures had been saved by Planned Parenthood. I called Dayna Farris-Fisher, a woman from Texas whose experience with Planned Parenthood had stuck in my mind, and asked her, "Is it okay if I talk about you?" She bravely agreed and wished me luck.

A couple of days before the hearing, we did a rehearsal so our team could explain how the room would be set up and demonstrate how things would work. There was a row of chairs, raised on a platform, like a judge's bench, and then a place for me in the front of the room.

"Who sits with me at the table during the hearing, so I can ask questions or get help?" I asked.

Lee Blalack, one of our lawyers, said, "I think it's better if you are up there by yourself. You don't need anyone."

I had a brief moment of panic. "Wait a minute," I said. "I've watched *Law and Order* reruns on TV. Everyone always has a lawyer!"

"You can do it. You'll be ready," Lee replied. Though I wanted to strangle him at the time, his confidence in me went a long way.

For our last run-through, the lawyers said I had to come in the clothes I would wear on the day of the hearing for a dress rehearsal, I guess. I picked out a basic blue suit and that sheriff's badge pin of Mom's. Whenever I'm up against something really tough, I bring Ann Richards with me.

**When you head into a tough challenge—an important game or performance or test—who do you "bring" with you?**

One of the young women associates looked me up and down. "If that's what you're going to wear, you should change your shoes," she said.

"My shoes?"

She pointed out that the pair I had chosen had a designer decal on the sole: ammunition for the opposition.

I hadn't even noticed. I don't think I actually bought the

shoes. I'm pretty sure I got them from Mom, who was much more fashion conscious than me.

It was hard to imagine having such a serious conversation with a male witness about what he was wearing.

The mention of my shoes was when I understood that I was going to be scrutinized from head to toe. That realization was later confirmed when the right-wing blogs went into a frenzy over the fact that I had not worn panty hose to the hearing. You have to look pretty close to see a detail like that.

At day's end there wasn't much more to do. I'd reread the facts and packed my binder. I'd steamed my suit again and set out a different pair of shoes. Kirk made us dinner. "Just remember," he said, "you know more about Planned Parenthood than anyone in that hearing room." I stopped to consider that; he just might be right.

I called the kids. Lily was in Iowa, where she had moved for Hillary Clinton's campaign for president; Hannah was in Indiana, working on a campaign of her own; and Daniel was in school in Maryland. They each wished me luck, and I went to bed early.

When I woke up the next morning I tried to meditate, as a friend had advised me to do. It didn't work. The team packed into a car and we headed to Capitol Hill. There were protesters standing outside the hearing, which was nothing new. It reminded me of a Planned Parenthood luncheon we'd had years earlier in a rural area. The place was difficult to find, and at the turnoff we'd had to drive past a group of protesters with ugly signs. Once we made it inside, one of our elderly donors, neatly dressed in her suit and pearls, approached me. "I saw those protesters outside," she said, and before I could say anything, she went on: "I was so glad they were there—otherwise I never would have known where to turn!" Remembering her made me smile.

Walking into the hearing room, I checked my phone one last time. I had an incoming text from a friend who wrote, "Just remember to carry the rage of women through the centuries with you this morning!"

During their speeches, I had quietly listened to the chairman and his committee members describe their version of women's health, the videos, and Planned Parenthood. Now it was my turn.

Chaffetz looked at me. "We will now recognize our witness. Please welcome Ms. Cecile Richards, president of Planned Parenthood Federation of America. Ms. Richards, pursuant to committee rules, all witnesses will be sworn in before they testify. If you will, please rise and raise your right hand."

I pushed back the chair, stood up, and smoothed my skirt. The room was silent except for the clicking of camera shutters. The photographers in front of me leaned in closer, so close they could rest their elbows on the edge of the desk. Bizarre as the experience was, they were a comforting reminder that somewhere beyond this room, people across the country, including my family and thousands of Planned Parenthood patients and staff, were watching on television and were with me. I raised my hand.

Preparing to testify before Congress.

"Do you solemnly swear or affirm that the testimony you're about to give will be the truth, the whole truth, and nothing but the truth?"

"I do," I said, smiling.

"Thank you," said Chaffetz, looking at me in a way I can only describe as sinister. It was a look that said *I've got you now!* I could feel how desperately he wanted to trap me. But I wasn't about to let that happen. Sitting there in front of the committee, seeing all the white men who mostly made up the Republican side, I didn't feel nervous, upset, or intimidated. I felt ready. I was overcome with a surprising sense of calm.

I took a deep breath and started my remarks. I talked

about the long history of attacks against Planned Parenthood that had been proven false and covered some basics about our patients. I ended with the experience of my friend Dayna: "Two weeks ago, I was in Plano, Texas, with one of these patients, Dayna Farris-Fisher. Dayna can't be here today because she has a new job and she's supporting her family, but if Dayna were here, she would tell you what she told me: that Planned Parenthood saved her life.

"In 2013 her husband lost his job, and therefore their health insurance. And not long after, Dayna found a lump in her breast. And the only two clinics that would take a patient without health insurance couldn't see her for at least two months. So Dayna came to Planned Parenthood for a breast exam. And there, our clinician of twenty-two years, Vivian, guided her through the process of follow-ups and referrals and helped make sure her treatment was covered. She called Dayna repeatedly to check on her treatment. And I am really happy to say today that Dayna is now cancer free.

"Mr. Chairman, I wish this Congress would spend more time hearing from women like Dayna. All women in this country deserve to have the same opportunities as members of Congress and their families, for high-quality and timely health care."

For all of Congressman Chaffetz's earlier emotion when he was talking about family members and cancer and his wife's job, he didn't even acknowledge Dayna's story. Instead, without a break, he launched into his first question, asking why Planned Parenthood funded work around the globe instead of focusing solely on the United States.

I started to answer: "Congressman, let me tell you—"

He immediately cut me off, shaking his head. "Oh no, no, no, we don't have time for a big narrative."

So that was how it was going to be.

After more rapid-fire questions and more interruptions, Chaffetz ended his remarks in time for a theatrical flourish, unveiling a slide.

The chart was labeled "Planned Parenthood Federation of America: Abortions up—life-saving procedures down." It had two arrows, in pink and red, neither of which related to the other. It was complete nonsense.

He asked me to explain the slide, and I told him I'd never seen it before. "I pulled those numbers directly out of your corporate reports," he said without hesitation.

At that moment Lee Blalack, seated behind me, leaned over and pointed out that a well-known antiabortion group had actually produced the chart. Its name was printed right on the slide.

"My lawyer's informing me that the source of this is actually Americans United for Life, which is an antiabortion group. So I would check your source," I told him.

Chaffetz was flustered. He ruffled some papers in front of him and his hands shook. "Then we will get to the bottom of the truth of that," he exclaimed, and turned to the next member of Congress who would question me.

His mistake helped me to realize, for the first time, how right Kirk had been the night before. This was my chance not only to defend Planned Parenthood but also to shine a light on the fact that many of the members of Congress who are the most obsessed with restricting women's health care know the least about it.

What followed was a stream of ridiculous questions. The minute I'd open my mouth to reply to their questions, the committee members would quickly shut me down, as if to say, *We are in charge here!*

The entire hearing was a painful display of the lack of interest in understanding the lives of the millions of women who turn to Planned Parenthood. Most of the committee members weren't there to get answers; they were using the opportunity to put on a show.

There were many choice moments. One of my favorites was from a congressman who clearly knew he and his colleagues were acting like fools. To try to rattle me, he said, "I'm sure I have seen many male witnesses treated much tougher than you have today. And surely you don't expect us to be easier on you because you're a woman?"

"Absolutely not," I replied. "That's not how my mama raised me." Silence.

Coming to his final question, the congressman tried again. "I'm not clear on this: Do you defend the sale of baby body parts?" he asked.

*Seriously?* "No," I said definitively.

In the middle of the hearing we took a short break. I checked my phone and happily saw a text from Daniel. He had been watching on TV and sent a note that only he could write: "Mom, you are really doing a good job. I think raising me all those years helped prepare you for dealing with these guys."

The break was over. It was back into the lion's den.

Near the conclusion of the hearing, Republican Congressman Trey Gowdy asked me if I understood the pro-life narrative. I replied, "I understand how people can disagree based on their religious beliefs, their background, their own personal experiences. And I also understand that people sometimes change over time and that's the human condition."

Gowdy looked at me with disgust and said, "I appreciate the way you try to frame these issues, that you're the reasonable one, and those of us who have a contrary position are not reasonable."

"I didn't say that," I said matter-of-factly. I knew he wanted me to take him up on his dare, and it made him absolutely crazy that I wouldn't. I clarified that I had never called him unreasonable.

"No, that's exactly the answer you gave," he said.

I reiterated that he'd gotten it wrong and restated my case, to which he finally replied, "It's not always what you say. It's sometimes just what you mean." Deep breath. Sometimes, when someone is making an idiot of themselves, especially on live television, it's just better to let them go ahead. I couldn't help but think to myself, *This is how Mom must have felt dealing with the old boys' club in Texas.* Like the time her opponent refused to shake her hand on the debate stage. Listening to their blustering and bullying, I realized that I had given them the opportunity to show their ignorance and hatred for women's health. That was almost more important than anything I could say.

Nearly five hours after we began, the hearing finally ended.

I couldn't believe I lived through it. The experience was utterly exhausting. I saw Congressman Elijah Cummings as I walked through the committee staff room. Congressman Cummings had made an impassioned speech in support of Planned Parenthood during the hearing. He had recently lost his mother-in-law to breast cancer, and now he stopped and looked me in the eye.

"I just think of all the women who, without Planned Parenthood, wouldn't get the care they need. Having just gone through this with my mother-in-law, I can't tell you how important it is to me."

I broke down in tears. His words had brought home exactly why we were there and why we had to keep fighting. I felt a combination of relief, exhaustion, and deep thanks.

Afterward I went back to the office and had a group hug with the Planned Parenthood staff. Though all I wanted to do was crawl into bed, I was scheduled to do a television interview. As I was walking into the NBC studio, my phone rang.

"Cecile, it's Hillary Clinton. I saw the hearing. You were wonderful. I'm going to be up there soon myself. Good for you for standing up to them." She would be facing the same committee in just a few weeks and spend twice as long, with much the same results.

For me, the experience was remarkable in many ways, but most of all, my respect for women elected to public office, which was pretty dang high already, grew by leaps and bounds after sitting through five hours with their colleagues. The sneers, interruptions, and plain rudeness are more than we would ever tolerate from our kids. But like so many women faced with a know-it-all who doesn't know much at all, they channel their anger and stay focused on what they're there to do.

At one point during the hearing, in the middle of a combative round of questioning, Congresswoman Tammy Duckworth spoke up about working her way through college as a waitress. "I couldn't get that waitressing job without getting a health exam. And I couldn't afford to go to a doctor. And the job said, you can start Friday if you come in with a valid health exam. Go to your local Planned Parenthood, they'll do it for you today, and you can start work in two days. It was a lifesaver."

I was proud but not surprised. In the many fights over Planned Parenthood funding, women have gone to the floor of Congress repeatedly and bared their souls about why Planned Parenthood is essential. Back in 2011 Congresswoman Gwen Moore from Milwaukee stood up and said, "I just want to tell you about what it's like to not have Planned Parenthood. You have to add water to the formula. You have to give your kids ramen noodles at the end of the month to fill up their little bellies so that they won't cry. You have to give them mayonnaise sandwiches. They get very few fresh fruits and vegetables because they're expensive." When she started talking, members on the floor were chatting and having side conversations. By the time she finished, you could hear a pin drop.

As part of that same debate, after hearing a male colleague's vicious antiabortion rant, Jackie Speier, a congresswoman from California, took the floor. She explained that she had planned to speak about something else, but the past few minutes had put her "stomach in knots." "I am one of those women he spoke about just now. I lost a baby," she said. "But for you to stand on this floor and to suggest as you have that somehow this is a procedure that is either welcomed or done cavalierly or done without any thought is preposterous."

I firmly believe that when half of Congress can get pregnant, we will finally stop arguing about birth control, abortion, and Planned Parenthood—and we might even fully fund women's health care. In the meantime, many women elected officials in Washington and across the country are doing their very best to stand up for an entire underrepresented gender. Time and time again they end up sharing their most personal experiences, just to try to evoke the slightest bit of sympathy from some of their male colleagues.

A few months before my appearance in front of the committee, I had read that a state senator in Ohio, Teresa Fedor, told the story of being sexually assaulted—raped—and having an abortion. She felt compelled to tell her story in response to a cruel bill in Ohio that would have banned abortion as early as six weeks—that's before most women even know they are pregnant—and would force women and girls to carry out pregnancies even if they had been sexually assaulted, or in cases of incest, when a family member sexually abuses a child. She hadn't talked publicly about her experiences before, especially not on the floor of the state legislature, but she mustered the courage to share her story even as her voice was shaking with emotion.

It was painful to think of the backlash she was likely facing, so I had picked up the phone and called her. I couldn't imagine what it took for her to tell her story publicly, and wanted her to know that I was grateful that she had been so courageous.

Here's what I learned sitting in front of the committee and from all the brave women who have spoken out: focus on the people who are counting on you, not the ones who are trying to drag you down. The Republicans on the panel wanted to provoke me into a fight, and the more I refused to get down in the mud with them, the more frustrated they became. But that was their problem, not mine. I couldn't control what they did, but I could control how I reacted. At the end of the day, I knew my patience and resolve could outlast their hysteria.

**Who is counting on you?**

And I'm glad to say that this story has a happy ending. Almost immediately after the hearing, Congressman Chaffetz announced that the committee had found no evidence of wrongdoing by Planned Parenthood (though that hasn't stopped politicians from continuing their efforts to block people from going to Planned Parenthood for care), and the committee disbanded. Later a leader and an employee of the Center for Medical Progress were indicted on fifteen felony counts. As for Chaffetz, he resigned his seat in Congress. Couldn't have happened to a nicer guy.

# 11

## All In

I could almost see Mom again, standing on the floor of the 1984 Democratic National Convention in San Francisco, waiting for Geraldine Ferraro to take the stage. That night Ferraro would become the first woman ever nominated as vice president on a major party ticket. "How does this feel, Ann?" a reporter shouted above the screaming delegates. Mom was not a sentimental person; life hadn't afforded her that luxury. But at that moment she was overcome, teary-eyed, as Ferraro's name was announced over the speakers. "I wasn't sure I would ever live to see this day," she said. "Finally, one of us."

Thirty-one years later, as Americans waited for Hillary Clinton to announce whether she would run for president in 2016, I remembered the look on Mom's face back then: full of hope, expectations, and wonder at how far we'd come.

\* \* \*

It would be almost a year between Hillary's announcement in April 2015 and the Planned Parenthood Action Fund's official endorsement of her presidential run in January 2016. Waiting backstage at Southern New Hampshire University in Manchester with dozens of our staff and patients, I saw Hillary come in through the back of the kitchen. Wouldn't you know, we were in matching navy-blue pantsuits. The second we saw each other, we both burst out laughing.

The audience was packed with Planned Parenthood supporters in pink T-shirts, and they were roaring to make history. Kicking off the event was a Planned Parenthood patient, Natarsha McQueen. Hillary listened closely from backstage. When Natarsha told her story of how an exam at Planned Parenthood detected breast cancer when she was just thirty-three years old and may have saved her life, Hillary put her hand over her heart. "Wow," she said.

When she took the stage, Hillary got straight to the point. "I have stood with you throughout my career, and I promise you this: as president, I will always have your back. I've been fighting for women and families my entire life. I'll go anywhere, meet with anyone, and work my heart out to find common ground. But I'll also stand my ground. I'm not going to let anyone rip away the progress we've made."

Listening to her, I felt a sense of wonder. When Planned Parenthood was founded, women didn't even have the right to vote. Yet after a hundred years we were endorsing a woman for president, and she was standing there thanking us.

Afterward Hillary headed backstage and graciously took a group photo with the team that pulled the event together.

Meeting Hillary Clinton at Planned Parenthood Action Fund's primary endorsement

(That photo is one of my favorites; several of the young women in it would spend the rest of the year working day and night to help elect her.) I introduced her to everyone as fast as I could, certain she would have to run. But she wasn't in any rush to get out of there. Rather, she made a point of thanking everyone, one by one. This wasn't her first election, and more than anyone she knew that these women—and millions like them—were going to be the heart and soul of her campaign. She wanted them to know that she appreciated their dedication.

By the time the Planned Parenthood Action Fund endorsed Hillary, the first contest of the presidential primary was only weeks away. Iowa is small, but its presidential caucus plays a big role in the campaign. The caucus process is so complicated, people spend their entire lives mastering it. Iowa was also where my daughter Lily was stationed, working on Hillary's campaign. So when Lily made a quick trip home for Thanksgiving, we begged her for a tutorial. She cleared a space on the dining room table and set up a demonstration about the candidates for the Democratic nomination. "Imagine these salt shakers are Hillary Clinton supporters. These pepper grinders are Bernie Sanders supporters. And these candles are Martin O'Malley supporters."

Over the course of months, the primary contest was going to work its way across the country, but the system was a convoluted patchwork, and that's putting it kindly. First, the number of delegates each state sent to the nominating convention in July would depend on, among other things, the size of the state's population. Big states with big populations, like California and Texas, sent more delegates than small states like Iowa and New Hampshire. But candidates showered Iowa and New Hampshire with attention because they held the earliest nominating contests, so whoever won them had momentum to go further in the race. Another twist was that each state had different rules and procedures for nominating candidates and assigning delegates. Many caucuses required people to gather in a room for hours and be counted on caucus night. States that had a primary election day with regular voting at polling sites all had different rules too—some were open primaries where anyone could vote, while others were closed, meaning only party members could vote. In those cases, Democrats had to choose one of the Democratic candidates, Republicans had to choose one of the Republican candidates, and independents were excluded from the process altogether.

I was excited about the caucuses, but I was even more excited at the prospect of traveling to Iowa to see Lily. I managed to organize my life so that every spare weekend or day off could be used to campaign for Hillary. When I walked into campaign central in Des Moines, Lily was in ripped blue jeans, Converse All-Stars, and a shirt I swear we bought her in junior high. The campaign office was a joyful wreck. My first thought was, *Can't we invent a more easily disposable pizza box?* There must have been a hundred of them scattered over the floor.

One of the things I loved about the Hillary campaign, much like Obama's in 2008, was the creativity of the volunteers, who had hung up yard signs and posters on every wall, in the shape of Iowa. I took a picture of Lily's desk; aside from piles of papers, it was littered with various treasures I'd gotten her over a series of campaigns: the sushi stapler, a small statue of the Hindu God Ganesha for good luck, desk monkeys, a photo of the Texas singer Lyle Lovett, and a bottle of generic ibuprofen.

Eventually we left the office and made our way to Lily's home-away-from-home in downtown Des Moines. Her apartment was a first-class disaster. I swung into action.

First, I washed all the dishes, then tried my best to gather up all the dirty clothes. (There's that skirt I've been looking for!) I did the laundry and threw out the dead flowers along with, yes, more pizza boxes. Just for laughs, I made the bed, knowing it would make not the slightest difference. But like all the other times when life feels out of control, doing the little things was enormously satisfying. I looked at her leather boots, which she wore daily—it was chilly in Iowa after all—and I just had to do something.

"I'm taking your boots to get polished," I announced.

"Ah, okay, Mom," Lily answered, sounding like, *Do you seriously think anyone cares how my boots look?* The next day I walked into Stan's Shoeshine Stand and set the boots on the counter. "Do you think you can rescue these boots?" I asked the elderly gentleman in the one-man shop, who I guessed was Stan.

> What rituals make you feel calm when things around you are hectic?

"Ma'am, I've polished the shoes of every presidential candidate since you were knee-high to a grasshopper, so I imagine I can get these in good shape! Just give me twenty minutes." I decided to go get coffee, and asked if he'd like some. "Black with two sugars, if you would," he answered. Like the rest of Iowa, he was "Midwest nice."

When I got back to headquarters, Lily had a phone in each hand and someone waiting to talk to her. Her feet up on the desk, she was in her element. I waited my turn.

"I'm finishing an event for Hillary late this afternoon, and then I'll get back to Des Moines by nine. Want to get dinner?" I asked.

She looked doubtful. "No way I'll be done by then, but maybe we can get coffee in the morning?"

I had forgotten the insanity of a campaign: eating

whatever you could, whenever you could, and having no other life. I managed to keep my worries to myself—about how little sleep she must be getting, the constant stress I knew all too well. But her boots looked great!

The key to the Iowa caucuses is that every county in the state matters, which means you get to see a lot of places that are really far away. I'm the kind of campaigner who will go anywhere—there's no meeting too small, no location too remote. It comes from my labor organizing days, knowing that around every corner there were amazing people you had yet to meet, and the farther from the center they were, usually the more grateful they were for the visit. That's how, just seven days before the caucuses, my colleague Suzanna and I found ourselves searching for a campaign headquarters in Conroy, Iowa, where the only landmark was an abandoned grain storehouse. Even the GPS couldn't help. Driving in circles, we finally saw a truck coming the other way, so I jumped out of the car.

"Hey there, hold on! Do you know where the Machinist Hall is?" I yelled.

The driver rolled down the window. "Yep, sure do," he replied. "Aren't you Cecile, Ann's daughter?"

How in the world? "Sure am! I'm out here campaigning for Hillary, and we're supposed to be meeting up with some folks."

"Well, me and the wife used to live down in Austin, and we retired up here a few years ago. I'm real glad for what you do—she's not gonna believe I saw you. Maybe we'll head over there too."

We got the directions, and sure enough, there was a tiny union hall just a few miles away, with a couple of pickup trucks with Hillary signs and "Proud to Be Union" bumper stickers parked outside. We carefully tiptoed through the ice. Though there didn't seem to be any heat inside the hall, there were a couple of dozen people of all ages and walks of life, sitting on folding chairs, waiting expectantly. Like every other campaign stop I made over the next many months, I was struck by all the young women running around, getting folks coffee, handing out phone lists for the area, and making sure everyone left with something to do.

Within an hour we were back in the rental car, speeding down snowy country roads in Iowa. I was scheduled to introduce Hillary at a rally in New Liberty later that afternoon, where I would get to see Lily and Kirk. Kirk was working with the labor unions and Lily was working the press, so this was going to be a rare mini family reunion in a suburban Iowa elementary school.

For the next eight months I would do hundreds of events, from phone banks in Colorado to house parties in Nevada, some with a handful of volunteers and some with hundreds. But that day, with Hillary there in person, was something truly special. It looked like every citizen in New Liberty had shown up. There were lines of folks trying to get into the school gym, as though the biggest playoff game of the season were about to begin. And backstage, as always, was the photo line. I'd never seen so many children, especially little girls, waiting to get their picture taken with the candidate.

*  *  *

After the rally in New Liberty, Lily, Kirk, and I made plans to meet up that night in Cedar Rapids, where I was deployed to campaign with the actor Tony Goldwyn. When we were done, Lily was waiting in the lobby of the hotel in town where the campaign was staying.

"Hillary wants to know if you and Dad want to get something to eat?" she asked. There was no way I was saying no to that. Before I knew what had happened, we were sitting down to a family dinner with Hillary, Tony Goldwyn, and a bunch of campaign staffers. The best part was seeing Hillary with Lily. Kirk and I sat there beaming with pride. Lily had started her life strapped into a baby carrier with me on union picket lines, and now she was a top staff member for a historic presidential campaign.

Our dinner conversation covered everything from the Iowa caucuses to how much my mom would have loved being there. Kirk talked with Hillary about the labor unions and their plans for turnout. There was no detail too small—she wanted to hear everything. When dinner ended, I was beat. I couldn't imagine how Hillary did it, especially since it was only January. My years of doing the same kind of schedule with Mom came rushing back, as did the protective daughter in me.

"Lily, you have to get her to bed," I said. "She cannot stay up like this and go campaigning again all day tomorrow!"

"Oh, that's nothing. She has to get up early for a TV interview in the morning." I was exhausted just thinking about it.

Though Kirk had to drive back to Des Moines, Lily and I stayed at the hotel overnight. As I was curling up in bed, completely spent, lights out, I saw the telltale glow of her cell phone under the covers. "What are you doing?" I asked.

"I have to check any breaking news so she's prepped for the morning," Lily mumbled.

The next morning her alarm went off at five, and she spent the next half hour scanning all the national and local news, trying to stay a step ahead.

The race was incredibly tight heading into the caucuses, but Team Hillary pulled it off.

"It was so close, but we won," Lily said first thing the next morning. "Turns out every single thing we did mattered. And listen—I've already packed up my apartment and should be getting to New York by next weekend." After nearly a year in Des Moines, my older daughter was going to work out of the Brooklyn campaign headquarters and live with us. The primaries were going to be a hard-fought battle, and Lily would be running press—working with the hundreds of reporters who reach out to the campaign—for the rest of the state contests, which were coming fast and furious.

# 12

## On the Road Again

By the time that Hillary had won the Iowa caucus, I had my campaigning go-bag packed and ready at all times, and I was eager to use it. For campaign travel, you need solid-color clothes (best for TV), whatever doesn't wrinkle, a hand steamer for emergencies, and sensible shoes. My trusty aide, a New Hampshire native and real political talent, Matt Burgess, became my traveling buddy for the next several months. He'd managed campaigns for governors and senators and knew the state of New Hampshire inside and out. Before our first trip together, I gave him a quick rundown.

"Okay, Matt, here are the rules. We never, never check a bag at the airport. We always carry our bags onboard, so pack light. Got that? And I'm always hungry, so your job is to make sure no matter what random town we end up at for dinnertime, we're gonna have something decent to eat. Tacos are a five-star when you can pull that off, though north of Virginia it might be hard." He nodded, a little dazed. And he went out and bought his own steamer that night.

Volunteering and traveling the country, I saw up close what a completely insane primary system we have and how challenging it is for voters in many states to participate. The states where voters go to the polls for the primary election have complicated enough rules, and to top it off, in states like Iowa that have a caucus system, people actually have to show up and literally stand and be counted for their candidate. That's tough to do for anyone who works a night shift or needs someone to watch the kids—namely, women.

A crucial state for Hillary, despite having a relatively small population, was Maine. I jumped at the chance to go, since it is almost an adopted home state for me. I'd gone to work in Maine as a nanny when I was a teenager, and I've been returning every summer. The kids were raised going to an island off the coast of Portland, and it is a place after my own heart. Give me a Maine woman any day. With so many cold months, they are scrappers, like my friend Sarah Meacham. They quilt, they crochet, they split wood. They can fix a tractor and know how to take wild apples and make thirty jars of sauce. Sarah taught me to make jam from wild raspberries and blackberries to last the year. Hillary reminds me of the Mainers I know, hardworking survivors who don't complain.

One afternoon Matt and I drove up to Kennebunk, Maine, for a house party, a small gathering of supporters and volunteers hosted at someone's home, right ahead of the caucuses. The host and hostess must have been baking all week; there were muffins and cheese sticks and stuffed mushrooms. After I gave my brief talk about Hillary, the local organizer explained how the caucus would work. "You are going to need to be at the school by seven," he said. "If you get there late, you can't participate. Then you should plan to be there for at least a couple of hours. And you are going to need to be ready to publicly state that you are caucusing for Hillary."

There was an uncomfortable silence. Finally an older woman spoke up. "We have a lot of Bernie Sanders supporters in this area, and they are really forceful," she said, sounding uneasy. "I'm so excited about Hillary, but I don't want to fight with my neighbors. We all have to get along here. It's a small town."

And so it went. A lot of our supporters didn't want to fight—they just wanted to be for Hillary. The attacks were coming from all sides, and many women felt they just could not speak up. There was an expectation that Hillary had to be perfect in every way. And when she couldn't possibly meet that unreachable goal, the critics were vicious. I had volunteered and campaigned for many less-than-perfect men running for president who didn't face the same scrutiny—this was a blaring and infuriating double standard. Just like with Mom, the attacks felt personal because they *were* personal. I tried my best to give pep talks to the women I met, encouraging them to talk to their friends and neighbors about why they were for Hillary.

**Has anyone ever tried to intimidate you? How did you handle it?**

If I had to do one interview, I had to do twenty where the reporter asked, "Why aren't young people for Hillary?" It wasn't true: young people did support Hillary, but it was tough to get that message through.

I was on enough college campuses during the primary to see how hard it was for a lot of the organizers and volunteers on Hillary's campaign. I also saw it firsthand with my daughter Hannah. We went out for coffee on a trip through Denver, where she was working. She had an enormous pro-Hillary sticker plastered on her laptop.

"I just figured I'm getting it out there," she said. Hannah was working with other young progressive organizers on environmental issues. "I get all these comments from the dudes in my office who are Bernie supporters, and I want to make a statement every time I flip open my computer. They aren't going to intimidate me." That's Hannah. As it turned out, Daniel felt the same way. I was glad they were able to support each other through a primary that got pretty unpleasant at times.

The primaries were hard-fought, but in the end Hillary clinched the nomination. As it turned out, the very next day she was scheduled to speak at the Planned Parenthood Action Fund meeting in Washington. All eyes would be on her.

Soon we were at the main stage of the Washington Hilton before a thousand cheering members of the Planned Parenthood Action Fund. I introduced her, and Hillary took the stage.

"Today I want to say something you don't hear enough: thank you. Thank you for being there for women, no matter their race, sexual orientation, or immigration status," she began. "Thank you for being there for every woman in every state who has to miss work; drive hundreds of miles; endure cruel, medically unnecessary waiting periods; walk past angry protesters to exercise her constitutional right to safe, legal abortion. I've been proud to stand with Planned Parenthood for a long time. . . . Because I know for a century, Planned Parenthood has worked to make sure that the women, men, and young people who count on you can lead their best lives—healthy, safe, and free to follow their dreams."

There were many firsts in the campaign, but one of them was that afternoon. It was the first time a nominee for the presidency had spoken without hesitation about her support for women's fundamental reproductive rights. By the time she finished, many people in the audience had tears in their eyes. For the next five months, the women and men in that room worked their hearts out for Hillary—people who had devoted their lives to reproductive rights and young activists who had just begun. The one thing that united them was Planned Parenthood and, in that moment, the opportunity to elect the first woman president.

The rest of the summer went much as everyone had planned, organizing phone banks and door knocking and training volunteers. Except for one thoroughly unexpected development: it became clear that despite all their best efforts, the Republican Party could not stop the momentum of Donald Trump. He was about to win the nomination at the

Republican National Convention in Cleveland, setting the stage for the most unpredictable presidential election in memory.

We made the Democratic National Convention, the formal event to solidify Hillary as the Democratic presidential nominee, a family affair. Kirk and Hannah and I drove to Philadelphia, passing car after car with Hillary stickers and people waving and honking. Hannah had never been to a convention and had agreed to travel with me for the next few days. I had to prepare a speech I would deliver at the convention. I also had to find an outfit that would be suitable for television, my mother's voice ringing in my ears: "Is that what you are planning on wearing?" Since, as has already been established, I'm not a fashionista, it was an enormous relief to find a navy-blue suit that would do. Plus, as always, I had Mom's gold sheriff's badge pin with me, and it was going right on the lapel. I couldn't get Mom out of my mind. This was what she lived for, and her spirit was definitely in Philly that week.

The night of my speech, Hannah went with me backstage to the makeshift hair and makeup studio where speakers were getting ready. There were about a dozen raised canvas chairs, makeup lights, hair dryers, and women everywhere.

There is nothing quite like speaking to thousands of people in a convention hall. It was impossible not to remember sitting on the stage, watching Mom deliver the keynote address in Atlanta to the same convention all those years ago. And unlike the convention floor in San Francisco in 1984 when the women were cheering for Geraldine Ferraro, tonight *everyone* was cheering for the woman we hoped would become president.

"When my great-grandmother was growing up, women couldn't vote under Texas law," I said. "Two generations later her granddaughter, Ann Richards, was elected governor. Tonight we are closer than ever to putting a woman in the White House. And I can almost hear Mom saying, 'Well, it sure took y'all long enough!'"

The night Hillary made her acceptance speech you could not have fit another body into that hall. Every young woman I knew was there. We were all proud of her, and proud to be part of history.

That entire fall was a blur of crisscrossing the country, going to phone banks to encourage volunteers, and speaking at college campuses to get out the vote. Everywhere I went, I met women I will never forget.

On the way from Silver City to Reno, a young woman from Chicago named Angelica Alfaro took us to a convenience store she swore had the best breakfast tacos in Nevada. She told me, "I ran for office last year, but the old boys' network rallied behind the guy in the race. I'm proud that I did it, and I'm not giving up." She had moved to Nevada just to work for Hillary and get more political experience under her belt. I expect to see her in Congress someday. In Traverse City, Michigan, I met a young woman who ran a volunteer phone bank. She introduced me to the crowd, which was how I learned her story. "I was homeless in high school," she stated. "Planned Parenthood was where I went for my health care, and with their help, I made it through school. And today I have a job working for Hillary. I'm on my way." No matter how tiring the road was, these women made me want to work that much harder.

Despite all the good energy, no matter how well Hillary did, it seemed impossible to break away from Trump. Every mistake he made on the campaign would have been the end of any other candidate. Like women (and men) across America, I felt sickened and disgusted when he was caught on a recording bragging about sexual assault. But nothing seemed to change the minds of his supporters.

My job was to remind women how strong Hillary was for them, and we knew that the Planned Parenthood Action Fund was the very best messenger for women voters. Which may be why the campaign asked if I could go to Las Vegas for the third and final presidential debate, ready to answer reporters' questions afterward. Both campaigns would have ten designated spokespeople to do interviews after the debate.

Hillary and Trump took the stage, so close to our seats I could practically touch them. Until that night I'd never seen Trump in person. For the next hour and a half, my anxiety rose steadily. Hillary was brilliant. But Trump was a disaster! He didn't have a basic grasp of how government works, and clearly no appreciation for the rule of law. He had no understanding of foreign policy, how our country relates to the rest of the world. It was obvious that if they pulled out a map and asked him to point to Syria, he would have been clueless. When he called Hillary a "nasty woman," I thought, *He is stark raving nuts.*

When it ended, it was obvious Hillary had performed spectacularly. That was the night that Hillary really broke away. Trump was clearly not fit to be president, and voters had seen it on the debate stage. Poll after poll showed she was in the lead. But I knew from my own experience how unpredictable campaigns can be. So even though I felt good, I never felt sure. That creeping dread was reinforced when the campaign asked me to go to Michigan and Wisconsin for the last two weeks. These were must-win states—was the campaign worried we might lose them?

"Folks just need shoring up," the field director told me. "And we'll have a final women's rally with Hillary ten days out in Cedar Rapids, Iowa."

"Great," I said. "We really have been needing to do something to energize women, and that sounds perfect." I figured there was no better high note to end on.

The rally was fun. The whole town of Cedar Rapids seemed to turn out. There were vendors selling Hillary T-shirts, folks who'd made Hillary jewelry and pins, and young girls wearing Hillary-like pantsuits. There were hundreds of Planned Parenthood folks in pink—girls, women, boys, and men. There wasn't a cloud in the sky—it was a perfect campaign day. Each of the speakers had her turn; then Hillary gave it her all.

But while the mood onstage was energetic and upbeat, behind the scenes was another thing entirely. Lily was texting me, but by then the news had spread. The FBI was reopening an investigation into Hillary's emails—had she done something wrong when she was Secretary of State and used a private email server? Like every other investigation of her, this would turn out to be nothing, but it dominated the news and made voters question their support for her. It was like watching all the helium leak out of a balloon.

During the next ten days we simply soldiered on. We knew our voters; we just had to get them to show up on Election Day. Everywhere we went there were young women working their hearts out. Back at the Planned Parenthood offices, I knew everyone was trying to stay focused and calm.

On the night of Election Day, I was back in New York City for what was set to be a huge celebration of the first woman president at the Javits Center, the biggest convention hall in the entire city. I phoned Kirk, who was still working the polls in Tampa, Florida: he never leaves the field until every vote is cast.

"I think we've done it. We hit the turnout numbers we needed in Broward County," he said. "And today's votes seem to be solid. If we win Florida, this is done."

Kirk is a crazy combination of realist and optimist. He's the one who believes until there is absolutely no hope left. He sounded pretty confident on the phone, but we'd both been through a lot of close campaigns and knew it could be a long night.

That night at the Javits Center was like a big family gathering. I recognized phone-bank coordinators from Iowa and folks who drove me around Colorado. Shuttling over to where all the media was set up, I ran into a reporter from

NBC News. "You must be feeling pretty good, Cecile," he said. "This is a big night."

Deep down inside, though, I wasn't feeling all that great. And with good reason. As I was preparing to do some television interviews, ripples were going through the Javits Center as terrible reports poured in from the states. It looked like Trump was going to win the election. I just couldn't bear to stay around any longer. A friend dropped me off at my apartment, and I immediately called Lily.

"It looks like we lost Pennsylvania," she said. She was keeping her emotions in check—she had to; she was working, having to talk to reporters from around the country. "Hannah called me from Denver. She is in really bad shape. Can you call her?"

"Yes, of course—but are you okay? Can I do anything for you?"

"No, just have to get through these next few hours."

I phoned Hannah, who was sobbing. "Oh, honey, I am so sorry," I said, now weeping myself. Nothing is more heartbreaking than trying to console your child, even if she is twenty-five.

"Mom, you have to call Lily!" she cried. "She's so upset." Each of my daughters was trying to figure out how to take care of the other.

The rest of the night we stayed on text, until finally it was clear it was over. I was emotionally and physically exhausted. Lily arrived at the apartment at four a.m. and got into bed with me, and we lay there and wept.

Kirk was on an early flight out of Miami, so he got home

a few hours later. We had faced devastating defeats before, and knew the only thing to do was to get up and keep going. Running on a few hours' sleep, I headed into the office. The night before, I had made a few phone calls to Planned Parenthood leaders out in the states. Today, there would be more calls to make, meetings to pull together, and intense planning to do. But most of all, I needed to make sure the staff were holding up.

When I got there, I walked by every desk on all three floors, checking in on people one by one. So many of the staff had worked so hard during the election, with some spending months out on the road. They were understandably distraught. I couldn't promise anyone that it was going to be okay—it wasn't. But I wanted them to know how much everything they had done mattered, to tell them we were going to get through this together. The work ahead of us was going to be as important as anything we'd ever done.

# The Resistance Is Female

JANUARY 2017

The flight from Miami to Washington, DC, was packed, despite the fact that we were leaving a balmy eighty-five degrees and headed straight to the cold. The mood on the plane was not at all what I'd expected: everyone was laughing, trading knitting tips, offering a spare room or a couch to traveling marchers. We had fought hard for Hillary Clinton's presidential campaign and we had lost. But we weren't dejected. We were determined. And we'd display our solidarity with our pink cat-eared knit hats. We were on our way to the Women's March on Washington, to protest the inauguration of a president who had bragged about attacking women.

I had finally finished knitting my hat after the third try, hell-bent on making my own at my local knitting store in New York City. As I sat there struggling with my needles and yarn, it wasn't hard to find help in a shop overflowing with women knitting. Some brought in hats they'd made at home to give away to folks who couldn't make their own. Mothers were teaching their daughters to knit, and people were in a joyful, revolutionary spirit. Everyone was leaving with a hat—one way or another.

On the plane, the flight attendant stopped to talk to me. "Do you think this march will make any difference?" she asked.

"I hope so," I answered, not really sure what we would find when we got to DC. Though I was beginning to get the feeling that the march might just be really big.

National Airport in Washington was buzzing when we arrived late that night. Women wearing knit hats and Hillary T-shirts were everywhere, greeting each other like long-lost sisters. I met up with Kirk at the hotel and unpacked my outfit for the march—black pants, black T-shirt, marching boots, and my bright pink blazer, on brand for Planned Parenthood.

The next morning the streets were already packed as I made my way to an early breakfast Planned Parenthood had organized for folks from across the country. After grabbing coffee, I gave a quick rallying cry to the breakfast crowd. I was preparing to head out when I spotted the granddaughter of an old colleague. The little girl beamed up at me with the most exquisite smile; she could not have been much more than seven, and she held up her multicolored hand-made sign that simply said, "I am a girl. What's your super-power?" *She is why we march today,* I thought.

Then off we went, with a crew of Planned Parenthood staff and others who needed a ride. Getting to the National Mall was nearly impossible, but we piled everyone into a van and drove as far as we could before hopping out and joining the streams of people heading down Capitol Hill.

We made it to the main rally stage and found a who's who of fierce women. Cookbook author and social media rock star Chrissy Teigen was there, and so was the great feminist icon and activist Gloria Steinem and the brilliant musician Janelle Monáe.

From my place onstage I looked out over a sea of pink knit hats for miles! "I'm honored to be here on behalf of the one in five women who has been to Planned Parenthood for health care," I shouted into the microphone.

A roar rose up from the crowd. The sound system was no match for the enormous gathering of people, but nobody cared. The stage stood near the National Mall, but no matter which direction you looked, you could see only marchers— all the way up to Capitol Hill and down to the Washington Monument. It was so packed that a lot of people couldn't even make it over to the actual march; they just plopped down on the grass to listen from wherever they were. And people just kept coming.

Later we would learn that the Women's March was the biggest demonstration in American history. But right then I knew only that it was one of the most beautiful sights I'd ever seen: people from all walks of life coming together for the right of working women to earn a living wage; the right of immigrant women who struggled to come to America from foreign lands to live without fear; the right of mothers everywhere to raise families in safe communities with clean air and clean drinking water; the right to live openly no matter who you are or whom you love; and, yes, the right of every woman to get the health care she needs. On that cold January day I was proud to be one of millions who poured into the streets to do my part for the resistance.

After I spoke, I pulled my pink knit hat out of my pocket and joined the march. I spotted Katy Perry in a pink faux-fur coat complete with sparkly pink boots and a pink "Stand with Planned Parenthood" pin. She and I and dozens of others took off for the Planned Parenthood gathering point.

There were so many people that the original plan to march to the Washington Monument just never happened. It was more like a virtual city, with spontaneous actions, singing, chanting, and celebrating.

And it wasn't just women—men marched too, including Kirk and Daniel. There were fathers marching hand in hand with their daughters, grandfathers who lifted their granddaughters onto their shoulders to see the crowd, and a whole lot of guys who were there simply because they want to live in a world where women are valued and treated fairly.

Best of all, people didn't march just in Washington. In every corner of our country people came together, grabbed homemade signs, and marched: in Fargo, North Dakota; Salt Lake City, Utah; and Des Moines, Iowa. They braved a blizzard in Fairbanks, Alaska, and marched in the rain in Tallahassee, Florida. In Boston even the *Make Way for Ducklings* statues were wearing tiny, carefully knitted pink hats.

And Austin, Texas, saw the biggest crowd gathered at the state capitol since a quarter century earlier, when Mom was inaugurated governor of Texas. People marched in every state in the United States and on every continent, including Antarctica, where women scientists at the South Pole held their own demonstration.

We each had our own reasons for marching that day. I marched for my mom and all the women of her generation who fought so hard to get us to this point; we won't let them down. And I marched for Lily, Hannah, and Daniel, and the future I so desperately want for them, one where everyone has the opportunity and the freedom to live life on their own terms.

Going to bed that night, I thought of what playwright Tony Kushner wrote in *Angels in America*: "The world only spins forward." Even though it still felt like our country was in free fall, those words rang true. The outlook was sure to be uncertain, and the next few years would pose one challenge after another, but we'd all have an opportunity to help shape them. No matter what else happens, nothing and no one can stop the future from coming.

After campaigning nonstop for months for Hillary Clinton, November 8, 2016, Election Day, was tough (to put it mildly). But the days right after the new Trump administration and the new Congress got to Washington were worse. It seemed like every morning there was some headline or tweet that made just getting out of bed feel like a radical act of defiance.

The Republicans now in control of the White House

and Congress signaled that they would repeal the Afford-able Care Act, and they intended to come down especially hard on Planned Parenthood. Our work was about to get a lot tougher, and supporters of women's rights were going to have to kick it into high gear. And they did.

Right after Republicans made clear their intentions, the congressional switchboard was jammed with calls. We could barely hold organizer trainings fast enough for the people who wanted to do something to help.

Meanwhile, Planned Parenthood staff across the coun-try were planning for different scenarios while working overtime to be there for a huge influx of patients. In the weeks after the election, our text/chat helpline was bom-barded with urgent questions. We saw a 900 percent increase in requests for appointments to get IUDs, a form of birth control that lasts for several years; women wanted to make sure their birth control would outlast the Trump administra-tion. We were doing everything we could to keep our doors open for the more than 8,100 people who count on Planned Parenthood each day, and trying to figure out what would happen if we couldn't.

In other words, everyone at Planned Parenthood was hoping for the best but preparing for the worst. We brain-stormed, planned, and made lists of anyone who might be a potential ally. We were heading into the battle of a life-time at Planned Parenthood. But for all my well-founded worries about what lay ahead for the women who depend on Planned Parenthood's care, I also knew that our greatest strength lay in their hands.

Members of the House of Representatives in Congress are up for reelection every two years. With our issues in the headlines, we wanted to make it clear that any member of Congress who voted to defund Planned Parenthood would be voting to take away health care from women who lived in their home district. It seemed like the best organizing idea was to get those women into the fight—and nowhere better than in the backyard of the most powerful congressman in Washington, then-Speaker of the House of Representatives Paul Ryan from Wisconsin.

Planned Parenthood has been providing health care in Wisconsin for decades, including at three health centers in Speaker Ryan's home district. So on a snowy day in February 2017, I flew to Milwaukee, picked up a car, and drove to Planned Parenthood in Kenosha, just three miles from Ryan's office. It's a typical, no-frills health center, and the center manager was there to meet us. Planned Parenthood health centers are always covered with photos of everyone's kids and pets, and this was no exception. They'd even put up a handmade sign out front reading, "Welcome, Cecile!"

We gathered together in the small waiting room. As the cameras rolled, three of our patients, Sophie Schaut, Gina Walkington, and Lori Hawkins, told their moving stories. Lori explained that she had turned to Planned Parenthood when she was a teacher at a Catholic school. One day she woke up with severe pain in her lower abdomen. Since she had a family history of cancer, she called Planned Parenthood. They got her in that day and found a large cyst and benign tumors on her ovaries. She was alone and scared that she'd never be able to have children. The clinician invited her to sit down, take her time, and use the health center phone to make the calls she needed to make. Lori made it through and now was happy and healthy and had two great kids. "Planned Parenthood made it possible for me to be a mother," she said, her voice filled with emotion.

Near the end of the press conference, Sophie said something that has stuck with me ever since: "I used to be a silent supporter of Planned Parenthood. But I can't stay silent anymore." Her words captured a theme that has been repeated over and over since the 2016 election: women who had never been involved were now becoming the fiercest, most passionate activists.

**Are there personal stories about yourself you feel shy about sharing? Do you ever think that sharing those stories might be helpful to someone else?**

Back in Washington, we decided to bring activists and patients to the Capitol, so that lawmakers could hear their stories before deciding whether to pull the plug on Planned Parenthood's funding, and all that it meant in the real lives of their constituents.

In March 2017 hundreds of people from all across the country converged on Washington, including Lori Hawkins from Wisconsin. This time she brought her thirteen-year-old daughter, Delaney, who told me she had insisted on coming with her mother. "I want to look Speaker Ryan right in the eye," she said, "and tell him that I would not be here if not for the health care my mom got at Planned Parenthood." I loved seeing these courageous leaders meet each other and get to know their members of Congress. The energy and solidarity of that day set the tone for what we would need going forward.

Two days later the Republican leadership released their health care plan, deceptively called "The American Health Care Act." Don't get fooled by a nice-sounding name. You've always got to read the fine print, the details in tiny letters that they don't want you to see. This bill would have made it much harder, if not impossible, and extremely expensive for women to see a doctor. And, sure enough, it would defund Planned Parenthood, meaning that women on Medicaid would no longer have access to the care Planned Parenthood provided. It was bad policy and it felt like an attack on women, which seemed obvious when a photo released from the Trump White House showed a room full of old white men proudly deciding that pregnant women didn't need maternity care. It reminded me of something Mom used to say: "You can put lipstick and earrings on a hog and call it Monique, but it's still a pig."

We went all-out with our message of opposition to the bill. We ran ads with our patients telling their stories. Every time members of Congress traveled back home to meet with constituents, Planned Parenthood supporters were waiting for them. Women always managed to track down Senator Lisa Murkowski at the farmers' market in Anchorage, Alaska, and thank her for standing up for Planned Parenthood.

In contrast, Congressman Mike Coffman from Colorado

was caught on tape running out a side door after a community meeting to try to dodge angry constituents. We had helped make the health care bill, or Trumpcare, as it became known, incredibly unpopular, and not a single member of Congress wanted to talk about it, unless it was to say they were voting against it.

And yet, because the House of Representatives was controlled by Republicans, the bill passed the House. The leadership celebrated snatching away health care from women with a party outside the White House, complete with nauseating selfies. The bill was now moving to the US Senate. If it passed that hurdle, President Trump would sign it and it would become law.

In the midst of this fight, we got some hard news out of Iowa. Because of a law signed by Governor Terry Branstad before he left office, Planned Parenthood was going to have to close four health centers. It was heartbreaking, and a preview of what could happen if Planned Parenthood were defunded across the country.

I wanted to hear what was happening on the ground, so I picked up the phone and called Angela, the health center manager in Bettendorf, Iowa. "How are you doing?" I asked.

She took a deep breath. "It's really tough. Patients are scrambling to figure out where they're going to be seen once we close. They're in shock, and they're angry. Some of them have nowhere else to go. Meanwhile, they're hearing politicians talk about them on TV, and the statements that are made about our patients—it's like facts don't even matter."

"What about the staff?"

"Oh, it's all the emotions you can imagine when you lose something you love. When the announcement was made that we would have to shut down, everyone was in tears. We had all lost our jobs. Someone said, 'Well, do you want to go home, and we can call the patients?' I said, 'No. I'm in this. I'm not going.' My staff said the same thing: 'Let's do this. Let's get ourselves together and see those patients.'"

By now I was barely holding it together. "Thank you for everything," I told her. "This is incredibly cruel, and the women of Iowa deserve better."

"You know, though, I wouldn't take it back for anything, my experience working for Planned Parenthood," she added. "I wouldn't give up a single day of being here. Even knowing what was going to happen, I wouldn't give it up for the world."

We said our good-byes, and I crossed my fingers that I wouldn't be making hundreds of similar calls because this bill had passed Congress.

Trumpcare was so unpopular, but in the Republican-controlled Senate, it was very likely to pass. I went down to Washington, ready to join my team and do battle. We didn't know who was with us, but we were doing all we could to shore up the women of the Senate. They had been clear: they would not support a bill that defunded Planned Parenthood. Our supporters flooded their senators with phone calls up until the very moment the senators filed onto the Senate floor to vote. There wasn't anything more to do on Capitol Hill, so I headed to my hotel room to sit and worry and wait.

The debate over the bill was a major nail-biter and went on late into the night. Senator John McCain of Arizona, who had just been given a tough cancer diagnosis, had been flown back to Washington so the Republicans would have enough votes. Would he be a yes or a no? He was a Republican, and no fan of Planned Parenthood, but was known to go his own way on certain issues. And when he literally gave the bill a thumbs-down, we knew he was a no.

The bill was officially dead. Chaos broke out on the floor of the Senate. Once again we had done the unthinkable. Hundreds of thousands of supporters of women's health care had beaten back the bill.

A few months later, the Republicans made one more attempt to pass the bill, but it felt like their heart wasn't in it. CNN held a nationally televised "town hall" meeting on health care—clearly, the debate over the issue wasn't going away. That night, a video clip came across my feed on Twitter. A familiar voice said, "My name is Lori. I'm a Planned Parenthood patient." It was Lori Hawkins from Kenosha, Wisconsin, on national TV! She looked the bill's sponsor in the eye and asked him why he would want to deprive anyone of the care she had gotten, which had made it possible for her to start a family. He answered in the most condescending way

**Do you realize that you have this kind of power? People power! How will you use it to help others?**

possible, even trying to explain childbirth—to a mother.

Yet again Lori made her very personal story public, because as hard as it was, she hoped it might make a difference for someone else. A few days later the bill failed again. I knew that our work was far from over, but the tally was Women 3, Trumpcare 0.

One of my favorite moments of 2017 happened on a trip to Arizona. The Phoenix Planned Parenthood office was filled with signs made for a town hall meeting that was occurring later that night in Mesa, Arizona. Their senator, Republican Jeff Flake, was a vocal opponent of Planned Parenthood. I asked the young organizers if they were ready to give Senator Flake a piece of their mind. They answered loudly, and without a second's hesitation, "Yes!" Everyone was giddy with excitement, but I couldn't help noticing one young woman in particular with a sweet smile and a resolute look in her eyes. Her name was Deja Foxx, and I had met her once before.

"Here's our plan," said another young organizer. "There are going to be hundreds of women there with our Planned Parenthood pink T-shirts on, so we are making sure a few of us are dressed in just regular clothes, to have a better chance of getting to ask a question at the microphone." Now that's an organizer for you! I wished them luck as I headed to the airport.

Later that night I got an email with the subject line "You have to see this." I opened the video inside and saw a determined-looking young woman standing up in front of a packed house, calmly taking the microphone at the public meeting while her senator watched from the stage. "I just want to state some facts," she began. "I'm a young woman, and you're a middle-aged man. I'm a person of color, and you're white. I come from a background of poverty, and I didn't always have parents to guide me through life. You come from privilege. So I'm wondering why it's your right to take away my right to choose Planned Parenthood." I leaned closer to the screen, and sure enough, it was Deja.

The crowd burst into applause that became a standing ovation. By the next morning, more than 12 million people had watched the video of Deja schooling her US senator. Since then she's spearheaded an overhaul of her school's sex education curriculum, traveled to Capitol Hill to defend her right to affordable, compassionate health care, spoken out on national television, and been featured in *Teen Vogue*. And today? She's a student at Columbia University, the first person in her family to attend college. That's the future of reproductive rights. Her generation—your generation—is the largest, most diverse, most entrepreneurial and open-minded of any generation before. More than 4 million young people turn eighteen every year in the United States—born troublemakers, naturals when it comes to questioning authority.

Women of all ages are leading the resistance. They're making organizing and activism part of their lives, bringing their kids along to town hall meetings, and signing up in record numbers to run for office themselves. In fact, a few months ago I got an email from a candidate training

The effort to stop the defunding of Planned Parenthood inspired organizers across America, including young women in Phoenix, Arizona, getting ready for a town hall meeting with US senator Jeff Flake.

program in Wisconsin, asking if I would recommend Lori Hawkins, who was thinking of running for office. Can you imagine how different our country would look if women like Lori, instead of men like Paul Ryan, were making decisions about the health care women need?

**What are the ways you inspire someone else?**

The fights we're facing—for affordable health care, equal rights, bodily freedom, and more—are never fully won. But the lasting legacy of this moment will be the generations of women it has inspired and energized.

# 14

## Everything You Need to Know in Life, You Can Learn on a Campaign (and Other Lessons Activist Kids Know)

My mother grew up in a time when most women didn't have many options; you could be a teacher, a secretary, a maid, or a nurse, and that was pretty much it. My kids, though, grew up seeing women in charge. Our life was such a matriarchy that when Daniel was three, he said, "When I grow up, I want to be a woman." He wasn't confused about being a boy—he was jealous. The women he knew were in power, doing important and cool things.

And yet, for my kids—and maybe for many of you— gender stereotypes were alive and well, subtly stifling girls and limiting their potential. The teacher in Hannah and Daniel's kindergarten class gave out "awards" at the end of the year. For the girls? "Most helpful to the teacher" and "Friendliest student." The boys' awards were very different: "Most likely to invent something" and "Best in math." It was maddening, part of a pattern we fought hard to break. And it's insidious, too, because the very qualities girls are expected to cultivate and are praised for—helpfulness, sweetness—make it that much more difficult for the women they grow into to demand their rights and make the powers that be squirm.

**Do you ever notice discrimination that is just below the surface?**

Here's a secret your parents probably don't want you to know: so much about raising kids is out of our control. I didn't know—and never quite figured out—how to get my kids to make good grades, keep their rooms clean, or stick with piano lessons. And while I certainly couldn't always control the stereotypes present everywhere from kindergarten to organized sports, I would always try to encourage my kids to question authority. The way things were wasn't the way things had to be.

Kirk and I were focused on the work of our campaigns, whether it was the labor rights of janitors, or Mom's race for governor, or defending Texas public schools, or reproductive rights. Our love for our kids was wrapped up inextricably with this work. The future we were fighting for was their future—so it was only natural to bring them along on our adventures, much the way Mom thought nothing of throwing my siblings and me into the back of the station wagon to go stuff envelopes for some long-forgotten Dallas city council race. Lily has said, "It never occurred to me that other people's living rooms were anything other than mass-mailing centers."

Along the way, it dawned on me that there are some pretty great takeaways from growing up around activism, beyond the goals of whatever movement you get involved in. These are some of the lessons my kids absorbed while knocking on doors, phone-banking, or just bantering with us about the news of the day—lessons that gave them self-confidence to chart their own paths and stand up for what they believe. Lessons that I hope encourage you to do the same.

## Family Life Is a Team Sport

Working as much as Kirk and I did was really for the best for everyone. When we moved to Washington, DC, in 1998, I didn't have a job. One day I sat all three kids down and asked, "What do you guys think about me maybe not going back to work? I could be here in the afternoon when you got off from school. We could do stuff together!"

They looked horrified. I'm sure they could count on one hand the days I had taken off from work to be with them, and the thought of my being at home was crazy. They had been raised to be independent and take care of each other, and they weren't interested in giving up their freedom. I certainly couldn't blame them for that. Besides, I think they knew, even at that young age, that it was in nobody's best interest for me to have extra time on my hands. So that answered that.

Kirk and I agreed from the get-go that we were going to take turns, and for the most part it has worked. At different points in our careers, one of us has been the one to work more regular hours, uproot their life for the other one's job, rush to pick up a sick kid from school. More often than not, it has been Kirk. I'm lucky to have found a partner who was willing to trade off with me like that. And, like in most families, our three kids were raised by a community of caregivers—family, friends, coworkers, babysitters, day care providers, and teachers—all of whom influenced them at least as much as their parents did.

One summer, when the twins were barely tall enough to see above the kitchen table, our friends Jennifer and Dawn were cooking hamburgers on the stove, something my kids had never seen, since I don't eat meat and do pretty much all the cooking. Hannah and Daniel peered up at the frying pan as if its contents were an exotic food from a foreign land and moments later sank their teeth into their very first burger. They cried out in unison, "Mom, you have to try this!" I like to think having so many people around all the time expanded their horizons.

## Everyone Picks Their Own Battles

My mom had a lot of rules to obey when she was a child, especially when it came to clothing. After a hardscrabble beginning, my grandmother was determined to make sure Mom fit in with the more well-to-do kids at her school. This included wearing the "right clothes." My grandmother had taken in sewing work during the Great Depression for extra money, and she made much of what Mom wore, making sure that the seams matched and that everything fit just so.

Mom carried on this tradition with me (I had those long wool skirts in college to show for it!). In keeping with her family tradition, on holidays Mom was hell-bent on ensuring that all three of my kids would be decked out in perfectly coordinated matching outfits, from their hats to their socks. When she was governor, it was hard to object when she wanted every child in a denim jumper with a matching red cowboy hat for the photos with the pony. At Christmas she would try to get them all in a photo looking nice. That lasted about three years.

The rest of the time I let them wear whatever they wanted. That resulted in some bold fashion choices, like Hannah wearing a pair of red cowboy boots with white stars nonstop for at least a year before moving on to a phase of tucking sweatshirts into her leggings. That's how she got the nickname "Tuck" from my friend Jennifer. Lily always wanted to have long flowing hair, which she did not. So she took to wearing elastic-banded skirts on her head, which was the closest she could get to golden tresses. This was a unique look when we went to the grocery store. And then there was Daniel, who wound up wearing little to no clothing pretty much whenever he felt like it. Why do boys like to run around naked and pee outside? I'm not sure, but that was his preference. There is an infamous photo of Daniel on an early camping trip, riding a bike and wearing only a helmet and sneakers. At least we did enforce necessary safety measures.

Beyond some basic standards, it was live and let live when it came to wardrobe decisions. I like to think it freed up some mental space for us all to focus on other things.

One of the other mantras drilled into me as a child was: you must try everything on your plate. Why? I have

no idea. But it seemed like a rule that I needed to pre-
serve in order to raise well-rounded children. There was
an unforgettable standoff between Daniel and me one evening, when I insisted that he at least
try the just-picked-from-the-garden
homegrown tomato at dinner. (If you
have not eaten a homegrown Texas
tomato, you must before you die.)
When Daniel refused, I was going to
show him who was boss! "Well then,
we are just going to sit here at the table
until you try it," I declared. The girls exchanged a *Who
does she think she's kidding?* look. We all ate dinner, and
everyone else finished. The rest of the family was excused
and went to wash up, but Daniel and I remained, locked in
a celebrity death match.

**Are there home
or school rules
you must follow
that don't seem to
make sense?**

Daniel was five, loved staying up all night, and didn't
have anything else to do. As far as he was concerned, this
was great. So we sat there for another two hours. Finally I
said something really stupid like, "Well, I have to go to work
in the morning to take care of the family, so we're just going
to see next time." In other words, I caved.

Daniel didn't gloat—he never was that kind of kid—but
he had definitely gotten the better of me. It helped me learn
that arbitrary rules are made to be broken, or at the very
least, questioned.

We tried hard to let the kids express themselves at an
early age and to challenge tradition and rules that exist
just because "we've always done it that way." This is how

they learned independence and to stand up for what they believe—even if they're standing up to a tomato.

## Get Comfortable Making Others Uncomfortable

I know all three kids secretly wished that at least once, on "career day" at Lafayette Elementary School, one of their parents was a firefighter or a librarian or something they knew how to explain to their friends. By that time Kirk was neck-deep in labor organizing and I was fighting for reproductive rights. We were always going up against some tough adversary, and the dinner-table conversation was usually about some injustice somewhere or our overwhelming frustration with the political scene in Washington. We were in constant battle.

One day Daniel came home and announced that his third-grade classroom had been talking about what they wanted to be when they grew up. He had decided he wanted to be a potter.

Daniel had not shown the slightest talent or interest in anything artistic. "That's great, Daniel!" I said. "What a fascinating thing to do. How did you decide that?"

"Because, Mom, nobody doesn't like a potter."

A little bit of my heart broke that night, and I realized that some of the toughest parts of life as an activist had gotten to him and his sisters. Daniel was learning that going up against the powers that be means there will always be someone who doesn't like what you're doing. That's the life Kirk and I chose. As a result, the kids learned that not everyone is going to love you, and that's okay.

Years later, instead of becoming a potter, Daniel headed off to Allegheny College in rural western Pennsylvania. He also became an activist and learned to stand up for his beliefs, which didn't always match up with the beliefs of his classmates or the campus administration. One of his proudest moments (and mine) was his fight to get reproductive health services on campus, as he was the vice president of Allegheny's reproductive rights organization. Daniel called me to say he'd met with the head of the school clinic. "We went in to talk to her, because, Mom, they won't even prescribe birth control for students, and it's hard to get it off campus." Eventually the campus agreed to provide prescriptions for birth control for students, a major win. That's my boy!

## Everything You Need to Know in Life You Can Learn on a Campaign

Lily never had a choice. At age three she went straight from janitors' picket lines in Los Angeles to the middle of Mom's campaign for governor. Our life was at work with her grandmother, or Mammy, as she called her. Letters to the tooth fairy were written on a typewriter in the campaign office, and she was probably the only preschooler who entertained herself by signing "Ann Richards" over and over again with the autopen machine. Though Hannah and Daniel didn't arrive until after Mom's election, they made up for lost time, as everyone around them either worked for the governor or on an issue on her agenda. By the time they were old enough to read, they were helping out at the Texas Freedom Network office, stuffing envelopes or making copies.

Campaign offices are chaotic places, and so was TFN; there were always volunteers dropping by, mailings to be sent out, or lists of people to call.

A campaign is a great place to pick up new skills. Early on, little kids can learn to alphabetize, since there is nothing like sorting a mailing list to nail the ABCs. And then there are the essential people skills. As Daniel, an experienced phone-banker, will tell you, people may not always be happy to hear from you if you're the twelfth call they have gotten reminding them to vote. Remaining cheerful, persistent, and well-mannered despite verbal abuse will always come in handy. And recruiting volunteers and raising money are skills you can use no matter your future path.

Every kid should know how to speak in front of people; even better if it's on the spot and you have to think fast about supporting a candidate or cause you believe in. When Hannah was in high school, she and I went door to door for President Obama during the final week of the 2008 campaign in Florida. It was an hour before the polls closed on Election Day, and Hannah had just one more door to knock on. The man who answered told her Barack Obama was born in Africa and was not getting his vote. Hannah's eyes welled up with tears as she explained that Obama was actually born in Hawaii.

"Well, I'm not going to vote for him anyway," he said, and stomped back inside. Nothing like a door slamming in your face to toughen you up.

Campaigning teaches you about putting everything on the line for what you believe in, and how sometimes you have to do the hard thing because it's right. No one thought Ann Richards could overcome the odds and become governor. The only reason she did was because she, and a bunch of others, never gave up. From her second campaign we learned that you don't always win, but it's worth the fight. And of course the greatest thing about working on campaigns, marching, and organizing is getting to do something important with people who share your passion.

One of my best memories is marching with my mom and kids in Washington with the Texas delegation at the national March for Women's Lives in 2004. Today there is nothing much better than seeing parents at a Planned Parenthood rally with a little kid in tow. I can't help but smile to think of the stories that kid will be able to tell one day about learning to take a stand even before they could walk. We learn best not from what we're told, but from what we see the people around us do, how they spend their days and what they do with their lives. I'm glad Lily, Hannah, and Daniel got to see early on that politics works best when it's not a spectator sport.

## Use Your Talents To Make Trouble Your Own Way

Having a mom who worked for Planned Parenthood came in handy for my kids more than once. At the very least, the kids and their friends knew they could freely ask about safe sex in our home.

It was also Planned Parenthood that provided the twins their first organizing opportunities. In 2011, when Congress turned on us and the efforts to shut down Planned Parenthood really took off in Washington, both Hannah and Daniel were in college.

Hannah called me from her dorm room at Wesleyan University, agitated. "Everyone at school is really upset about this defunding of Planned Parenthood, but I don't really know what to do. We just have to do something."

"Students all over the country are getting involved right now. How about you organize something on campus?" I suggested.

We hung up, and the next week I got a notice that the students at Wesleyan were holding a rally of support for Planned Parenthood. I knew right away: that was Hannah. She'd just gotten it together—created a Facebook event, hung posters around campus, told everyone she knew, and remembered to call some reporters a day or two before the event. Hundreds of people packed into a hall on campus, plus overflow rooms.

Senator Richard Blumenthal and the university president even showed up to speak. After the rally, a bunch of Wesleyan students made an amazing video in support of Planned Parenthood, titled "I Have Sex"—you better believe it went viral.

Daniel knew what was happening from the news, but that was about all I was sure of. One Saturday I was racing downtown in New York to speak at a Planned Parenthood rally when I got a text. "Hey, Mom, I'm in a car with some kids from Allegheny. We're driving to Ohio to a rally for Planned Parenthood. I love you." It was from Daniel.

My first reaction was totally emotional: here was my happy-go-lucky son, getting in a car to spend his weekend fighting for Planned Parenthood. But my second thought was *Wow, if Daniel is driving to Ohio, then this is a movement, and we are going to win.* (Which we did, thanks in no small part to young people who organized on campuses across the country.) Today Daniel is a chemist, but also a lifelong political activist, and proud of it.

As for Hannah, she's worked as an organizer on environmental issues and reforming our gun laws, among other causes. If anyone is taking up the family business, it's her. She's experienced the pains of coalition building just as Kirk and I did when we were trying to organize New Orleans back in the day. How do you get groups to see their shared interest on some issue when they may have nothing else in common? Every now and then I get a call from her ahead of some big community hearing or after an organizing mishap, and my heart skips a beat. We are constantly brainstorming organizing strategies, and I wouldn't have it any other way. I have such enormous love and respect for her.

And Lily? Well, she picked up where her grandmother left off. I tease her that her public profile peaked at age one and a half, when Mom mentioned her in the Democratic keynote speech in Atlanta. That night Kirk was wandering around the convention hall, wearing a homemade button that said "Lily's Dad." Mom, meanwhile, was eager to pass on all the important life skills she had spent years learning: If you can't remember someone's name, you can always call them "honey." Never wear patterns on TV. And for heaven's sake, before you name your kid, think about how it will look on a bumper sticker or billboard.

Lily remembers those Ann Richards lessons like nobody I know, and they've served her well in politics. She's worked for US senators, worked on campaigns, won and lost. And who could have guessed that her early experience at Baylor University would turn out to be such good training when, in her twenties, she found herself a target of Rush Limbaugh, the right-wing radio host? Limbaugh had made some ugly comment about women's bodies, and Lily, who was working at the Democratic National Committee, sent an email calling on Republican leaders to stop going on his show. Next thing we knew, Rush was yelling about Lily Adams, even reading her email on the air in a mocking little-girl voice. Lily was unfazed; she couldn't believe he took the bait. When I asked her how getting attacked made her feel, she said, "It's just the cost of doing business. . . . At the end of the day you just have to stay grounded and, you know, keep doing what you're doing. Mammy used to say that seeing a dried egg on a plate in the morning is a lot dirtier than anything she'd seen in politics."

The best is when we all join forces for a cause. President Obama's historic campaign in 2008 was a family project. All three kids volunteered, even though the twins weren't old enough to vote. Like millions of other young people, they got a front-row seat to the power of grassroots organizing and the importance of elections. Kirk and I and the kids were scattered across the country in the last week of the campaign. On Election Day, Hannah and I were in Florida,

Lily was door knocking in New Hampshire, Kirk was in Virginia, and Daniel was back home in New York City. Every few hours Kirk managed to organize a family-wide check-in to compare notes. I'm not sure how many other families were getting on a recurring conference call that Election Day. On our last call of the night, when we realized Obama had won, Daniel ran out into the streets of New York City with thousands of others to celebrate. Of all the marches and campaigns we've done as a family, nothing will ever match being at Obama's first inauguration together, watching history unfold.

We were back at it in 2012, each of us in a different state for Obama's reelection campaign. Lily was working on a senate race in Virginia, and I wound up in Richmond, Virginia, on Election Day to help get out the vote. A friend and I spent the day phone-banking as if our lives depended on it. After we got through our call lists, we headed out to knock on doors in the suburbs, where women were getting their neighbors to watch their kids so they could run over and vote after work. As the polls closed, we stopped at campaign headquarters to check in on Lily.

"We finished our walk lists and phones calls—is there anything else we can do?" I asked.

Lily looked around. "Is there anything else?" she called over to the field team.

"Well, there are a few polling places where people are still outside, waiting to vote," someone answered. "The election officers have to keep the polls open if folks are in line."

Before they could finish, my friend and I were getting

our coats on. First we headed to the closest Krispy Kreme and bought ten dozen doughnuts and some boxes of coffee. Then we drove to the closest polling place, where we poured coffee and handed out doughnuts to the people who were standing out in the cold, waiting for their turn to vote. They were elderly folks, women with kids in their arms, students doing their homework as they held the line. We sent a picture back to Lily at the office. It was the perfect election night.

## There Are Some Basic Life Skills We All Need, Whether or Not We're Activists

Kirk and I have been really lucky. Despite the fact that our kids grew up on picket lines, in campaign offices, and at day care—or, I like to believe, because of it—they're good people, and each is working in their own way to make a difference. They are funny and kind, and they are patient with their parents, who have often put organizing ahead of clean clothes or sitting down for dinner at regularly scheduled times, and they have the basic life skills that are necessary for survival and joy.

I imagine your parents feel as I do: the control we lack gives way to hope, the hope that you kids have the confidence and opportunity to follow your own path in life—to take risks and do what makes you happy. And if, in the meantime, you change the world along the way, so much the better.

One of countless adventures with Daniel, Hannah, Lily, and Kirk.
Cape of Good Hope, 2016.

# EPILOGUE

## "Feminist" Is Not a Passive Label

So now what do I do?"

It's a question I've been asked almost every day since the 2016 election, by everyone from corporate CEOs to a young woman on the subway last week to a fourth grader who I met recently in Nashville, Tennessee ("Run for class president!" I suggested). What they're really asking is, *Now that we can no longer take for granted that America will slowly but surely make progress, our entire world seems to be spinning out of control, and we're fighting tooth and nail to protect our most fundamental rights—how do we make it all better?*

Great question, and not one to which I have a neat and tidy answer.

But here's what I do know: there has never been a better time to become an activist, agitator, or troublemaker. I promise you, doing something—whether it's showing up at a town hall meeting, getting some friends together to start your own organization, or just refusing to keep quiet about what you believe—feels infinitely better than sitting on the sidelines. Looking back on my life so far, the moments I regret most are the ones when I was too scared to take a chance—the moments when I didn't know what to do, and so did nothing.

In some ways, being an activist in public is easy; standing up for yourself in your own life can be much harder. Even after years of loud and proud troublemaking, I've found myself in situations where I was too fearful to speak up for myself. There was the summer job in college when my employer touched me inappropriately, yet I was terrified of losing the opportunity to learn from him, so I never said anything. Like so many women, I can remember every single detail forty years later. I don't want that to be the fate of my daughters or any other girl.

Then there was the conversation about a job in Washington where my future employer said, "I know you have three kids at home, so maybe you just want to work part-time?" "Nope," I replied. "I need this job, and my husband and I are both working full-time." It wasn't until later that I found out my "progressive" employer was paying my male colleague, working the same job, nearly twice what I was earning. Why didn't I think enough of myself to raise hell at the time?

Now the floodgates are open. Women are talking publicly about subjects that were once off-limits, and there's no going back. As Mom used to say, "You can't unring a bell." It shouldn't be up to women to dismantle the patriarchy, but we can't sit around and hope someone else does it either.

*Feminist* is not a passive label; it means speaking out and standing up for women everywhere, and also for yourself. One woman calling out an injustice is powerful enough; when we raise our voices together, we can shake the status quo to its foundation.

For activists and troublemakers, especially now, there's no shortage of fights to take on. I've been proud to be part of the movement for reproductive freedom for over a decade, and to have invested in bringing a whole new generation of leaders into the fold. I believe it's time for one of them to take over, which is why I decided to leave Planned Parenthood after twelve years and turn to the next chapter—in our movement and in my own life. It wasn't an easy decision to make—leaving a job you love never is—but I am confident it was the right one. And now I'm back to political organizing, but with a twist. I'm working with some incredible leaders to start a new organization called Supermajority dedicated to building women's power and expanding women's civic participation.

Now more than ever, women are the most important political force in America. We have enormous power to change the direction of this country, and it's time to use it. Marching, knitting, and protesting are great. But voting, and changing who is elected to office, is essential.

No matter where I have gone since the 2016 election, I have run into women who are organizing like never before. On one campaign swing through Ohio, you couldn't throw a rock without hitting a newly formed grassroots women's group—from the Matriots, a statewide group dedicated to electing progressive women, to a group in Cincinnati started by a local woman to confront the epidemic of death during childbirth among black women. My daughter Hannah summed it up so perfectly when she said, "You know, out here in Colorado there are so many new women's groups . . . but you don't really see new *men's* organizations!" She had a point. It was clear to me that women everywhere were longing to come together, to take action, to shake things up.

And yet. Overwhelmingly, women recognized that politics is not an easy arena to jump into. "I had to read up on how to even run for the school board," said Dionna Langford, now on the school board in Des Moines, and the only African American member. "No one was there to help me figure it out." Down the road in Cedar Rapids, a longtime political activist looking ahead to the midterm elections said, "I'm going to volunteer to phone-bank and knock on doors again this year like every year. But it's frustrating to know I'm working in a system built by men, for men."

She's right. Wouldn't it be great if employers stopped treating pregnancy like a nuisance and started treating it like the basic reality it is for millions of workers? Maternity benefits and child care might actually be seen as—dare to dream—necessities for growing our economy. Public school teachers wouldn't have to strike to get attention to education needs for our children. We could have a government that actually supports families instead of tearing them apart. And most importantly, issues that women care about could finally be understood not as distractions but as fundamental issues of fairness and dignity that everyone should care about.

The most profound leadership we're seeing today isn't coming from the halls of government—it's coming from women at the grassroots. And in the 2018 midterm elections, a record number of women, and women of color, ran for office, and we saw why it all matters.

Women ran for office to change the world—and won. Women like Lucy McBath in Georgia, a mother who lost her son to gun violence. She realized the criminal justice system is broken, and it is her passion to fix it. She's now a congresswoman. Or Angie Craig from Minnesota, whose congressman made such hateful statements about LGBTQ people that she decided to take him on. And she won. Now she's the first lesbian mom in Congress. Or Lauren Underwood, a registered nurse in Illinois, who sees every day what it means when people don't have access to affordable health care. She challenged six men in her political primary, then went on to win the election and is the youngest African American woman in history to serve in Congress.

Across the country, women have challenged conventional wisdom and odds and re-created politics the old-fashioned way—by knocking on doors, meeting their constituents, and often by outworking their opponents. I'll never forget the photo candidate Alexandria Ocasio-Cortez posted of her shoes, literally worn to the soles from walking neighborhoods to meet voters. Now she's the youngest woman elected to Congress. And then there's Anna Eskamani, who ran for office in Florida. She spent a year with a clipboard in her hand, knocking on doors, talking to everyone she possibly could about why she was running. When she found herself on the receiving end of attack ads and smears, she shrugged it all off and kept going. And now, at twenty-eight years old, she was sworn in as the first Iranian American ever elected to the state legislature in Florida. Can you imagine how different our world will look when governments around the world are filled with women like Anna, Alexandria, Lucy, Lauren, and Angie?

The women who come through the doors of Planned Parenthood health centers every day have a lot on their minds, like men and women all over the country. Above and beyond getting affordable, nonjudgmental health care, they want a safe neighborhood for their kids and an excellent public school system. They want to earn a living wage, and work without facing harassment or abuse. They want family leave and affordable child care. They want to live in communities free from gun violence. They deserve all this and more, and that's what I'll keep fighting for.

Sometimes I picture my thirteen-year-old self, getting on the school bus, wearing that black felt armband, preparing to embark on a lifetime of making trouble. There's so much I wish I could tell her: Stay strong even when people criticize or doubt you. Every meaningful relationship, every friendship, and the love of your life will come from standing up for what you believe. The world can be tough, unjust, and even cruel, but you have the power to do something about it—at any age. We all do. It's not about having it all, doing it all, or being perfect—it's about getting started.

There's a poem I always seem to find my way back to: "The Low Road," by Marge Piercy. Part of it goes like this:

> *It starts when you care*
> *to act, it starts when you do*
> *it again after they said no,*
> *it starts when you say We*
> *and know who you mean, and each*
> *day you mean one more.*

So here's to the troublemakers, the agitators, the organizers. This is our moment.

# Acknowledgments

Going through the last six decades has involved a lot of people, and I'm forever grateful to everyone who has helped reconstruct years of adventures in troublemaking. Thank you to my friends from the labor movement, the Planned Parenthood family, Capitol Hill, and elsewhere for your memories, editing, and guidance: Debra Alligood White, Peter Brownlie and Deborah Jenkins, Matt Burgess, George Crawford, Diane Dewhirst, Brendan Daly, Congresswoman Rosa DeLauro, Anna Eskamani, Roger Evans, Marisa Feehan, Eric Ferrero, Yvonne Gutierrez, Amanda Harrington, Lori Hawkins, Jane Hickie, Maryana Iskander, Rebecca Katz, Jennifer Kinon, George Kundanis, Ken Lambrecht, Dawn Laguens, Dutch Leonard, Chuck McDonald, Nick Merrill, Laura Olin, Selena Ortega, Democratic Leader Nancy Pelosi, Janis Pinelli, Lynne Randall, Callie Richmond, Steve Rosenthal, Laurie Rubiner, Jen Samawat, Dan Schwerin, Jono Shaffer, Dana Singiser,

Evan Smith, Andy Stern, Emily Stewart, Sarah Stoesz, Tom Subak, Luis Ubiñas and Deb Tolman, Sarah Weddington, Brady Williamson, and Liz Zaretsky.

Thank you to the Ann Richards campaign family, who raised my kids and taught us all what it means to dream big. Thank you to the hundreds of nursing home workers, janitors, hotel staff, and more whose courage to fight for justice continues to inspire me. In the words of Nelson Mandela, "It always seems impossible until it's done." And, of course, thank you to Hillary Clinton for giving me the honor of traveling the country to support your campaign. When we elect the first woman president of the United States, it will be because of you.

This book, and my life, are better because of the friends who have stuck by me and encouraged me every step of the way: Patti, Annette, Rebecca, Gina, Samantha Smoot, and many more.

Thanks to our editor, Ruta Rimas, and the team at McElderry Books, including Nicole Fiorica, Karen Wojtyla, Justin Chanda, Anne Zafian, Bridget Madsen, Lauren Rille, Vikki Sheatsley, Tatyana Rosalia, and Audrey Gibbons; to Meg Thompson and Cindy Uh at Thompson Literary Agency, who helped us on our first book adventure; and to Robin Gaby Fisher, for your infinite patience and for making this possible.

None of this would have happened without the partnership with Lauren Peterson, who believed we could write a book, and then we did. Her commitment to telling this story, and to doing it with me, is a gift I can never repay. Thanks for writing your first book with me—as Lin-Manuel Miranda would say, "History has its eyes on you." Thank you also to the extended Collins-Peterson clan for copyediting, moral support, and for getting us across the finish line.

Thank you to Ruby Shamir for the wonderful work she did adapting this book for young readers, and to Eugenia Mello for her enthusiasm and beautiful cover art.

You are holding this book in your hands because of the generosity and support of my incredible family. Thank you to Dan for unearthing hilarious political cartoons and swapping stories; Ellen and Greg for discussing campaign life and child-rearing over breakfast tacos; Clark for being my attorney and adviser and great brother. And of course, thanks to Dad for your wisdom and recollections and for teaching us kids about justice and progressive values from an early age.

Hannah, Daniel, and Lily were invaluable collaborators with an uncanny knack for remembering some of our best (and funniest) moments as a family. I am so proud to be your mom. Thank you, Kirk—for your eagle-eyed copyediting, for walking Ollie, and for being my biggest cheerleader and partner in troublemaking all these years.

And to the thousands of organizers and activists without whom there would be no story: thank you.

# Photo Credits

p. 46: Alan Pogue

p. 51: Iris Schneider

p. 60: Ave Bonar

p. 66: Ave Bonar

p. 145: Callie Richmond

p. 163: Mark Wilson/Getty Image News Collection/Getty Images

p. 174: Barbara Kinney/Hillary for America

All other photographs courtesy of the author

# Index